Alfred Worcester, William Atkinson

Small Hospitals

Establishement and Maintenance, and Suggestions for Hospital

Architecture

Alfred Worcester, William Atkinson

Small Hospitals
Establishement and Maintenance, and Suggestions for Hospital Architecture

ISBN/EAN: 9783337161262

Printed in Europe, USA, Canada, Australia, Japan

Cover: Foto ©ninafisch / pixelio.de

More available books at **www.hansebooks.com**

SMALL HOSPITALS.

ESTABLISHMENT AND MAINTENANCE

BY

A. WORCESTER, A.M., M.D.

AND

SUGGESTIONS FOR HOSPITAL ARCHITECTURE.

WITH

PLANS FOR A SMALL HOSPITAL.

BY

WILLIAM ATKINSON, Architect.

NEW YORK:
JOHN WILEY & SONS,
53 East Tenth Street.
1894.

PREFACE.

MANY times within the last few years it has been my privilege to address audiences in neighboring communities where the hospital movement was under consideration, and to meet visiting committees who had come to study the methods and plans of the one hospital which I have had the pleasure of seeing grow from nothing into its present condition of usefulness. At such meetings the impossibility of even briefly telling the whole story has always been an embarrassment. And now in this attempt to tell it I have the pleasure of hoping to help others to the fruition of their endeavors.

This hope has been greatly enhanced by the addition of Mr. Atkinson's admirable description of the model hospital from the architectural standpoint.

A. W.

WALTHAM, MASS., June, 1894.

CONTENTS.

Part I.

CHAPTER I.
PAGE

The New Hospital Movement. Its Origin. Advantages of Small Hospitals to the Community 1

CHAPTER II.

How to Interest the Public. Preliminary Meetings. Selection of Committees 12

CHAPTER III.

Hospital Organization. The Corporation. The Board of Managers. By-laws. The Executive Committee . 21

CHAPTER IV.

The Medical Question. Homœopathy and Allopathy. Possible Solution of the Difficulty. The Selection of the Staff. Charges for Professional Services to Hospital Patients 29

CHAPTER V.

The Nursing Service. Establishing a Training School. Selection of a Superintendent. Probationers and Student Nurses 41

v

CHAPTER VI.

The Temporary Hospital. Transformation of Dwelling-house. Temporary New Wards. Cottage Ward for Contagious Diseases. Furnishings. The Ambulance   53

CHAPTER VII.

The Admission of Patients. Necessary Regulations   . 65

CHAPTER VIII.

The Permanent Hospital Buildings. How to Plan and how to Build them   71

CHAPTER IX.

Hospital Finances. Hospital Aid Associations. Hospital Sunday and Saturday Collections. Endowments. Free Beds. Public Appropriations   79

Part II.

HOSPITAL ARCHITECTURE,   91

SMALL HOSPITALS.

CHAPTER I.

THE NEW HOSPITAL MOVEMENT.—ITS ORIGIN.—ADVANTAGES OF SMALL HOSPITALS TO THE COMMUNITY.

WITHIN the last few years small hospitals have been built in many of our larger towns and smaller cities, and where this is not already accomplished steps thereto have been taken. Indeed, so rapidly is the movement progressing that it seems as if even the smaller towns would soon be planning each to have its own hospital. It is a striking instance of our advancing civilization. Before the war there were hospitals only in the largest cities. During the war and the few following years these institutions, in spite of the existence of the great temporary hospitals, were frightfully overcrowded. It would seem natural, therefore, to find in those years the beginning of the popularity of the hospital movement. But it was not then. Although the army surgeons and hospital stewards carried back into their peaceful lives a knowledge of the worth of hospitals for the results of violence, they as yet saw no advantage in them to an ordinary community.

These men knew how to build and equip and carry on a hospital, but they did not know nor did any one know how to prevent the occurrence of hospital fever, or, in more exact words, the various forms of blood-poisoning. It is terrible now to recall the ravages even in late years of septicæmia, not only in hospitals, but in the homes of the rich as well as of the poor—terrible, because it was preventable. Words cannot be found in which to express the gratitude humanity owes to the discoverers of the vegetable origin of these diseases and of the methods of destroying these bacteria. It is here, in the discovery of the prevention of blood-poisoning, that we rightly find the beginning of the new hospital movement. No longer could it be said that any patient would be safer in his own home, even if on a mountain-top, than in the hospital. Indeed, so perfect has become the germ-defying *régime* of the modern hospital, that it can be truly said a patient is there less exposed to the danger of blood-poisoning than he would be in any private home.

The old disadvantage thus swept away, nothing was left to weigh against the manifold advantages which can be furnished to a community by a hospital. None were so quick to recognize this as the old army surgeons and hospital stewards. You will find them on every hospital staff and governing board, and on the committees of supply you will find women whose hands have rolled bandages and scraped lint in the dark days thirty years ago.

Not in one direction alone are we ever to seek for the cause of a general advance. Hospitals are everywhere springing up, not merely because their advantages were made so apparent in war times, nor only because the germs that formerly killed have themselves met their destroyer. An even greater cause is to be found in the development of the art of nursing.

Trained nurses can now be had in almost any community; and yet there was not one in this country at the breaking out of the last war. Nor were there any really trained nurses for some years after the war. Dreadful as was the nursing in private homes, in hospitals it was simply atrocious. In the Bellevue Hospital of New York, for instance, the nursing was formerly entrusted to women who in the police courts chose a term of service as hospital nurses when the alternative of a term of imprisonment was given them. No wonder that these nurses would occasionally be found drunk by the deathbeds of their neglected patients, whose stimulants they had stolen. Now in the same hospital the nursing is done by intelligent, cultured women, who almost give their services for the education there obtained. And the profession of nursing having supplanted the vile trade of last resort, rightly shares with the profession of medicine the highest honor and glory. Graduates of the various training schools are now at hand to take charge of the new hospitals and to carry on not only the hospital work, but also the work of training other nurses, who in their turn will extend the same blessings into ever widening fields.

Surely it is to this development of the profession of nursing that the rapidity of the new hospital movement is most largely due. Among other causes is the great advance of recent years in surgery. Owing primarily to the discovery of germicides, and of the means of preventing the access of germs to wounds, surgeons have been enabled to operate without danger to the patient's life in regions of the body formerly inaccessible because of the peril involved. An abscess, for instance, may arise in any part of the body. In former times if the abscess was located near the surface or in one of the limbs the patient's life was not seriously threatened: if, however, the abscess was inside the body proper,—in the skull, the chest, or the abdominal cavity,—then it was considered out of the surgeon's reach, and the victim was doomed. Now the skull, the chest, or the abdomen can be safely opened, and the destroying pus evacuated. But such operations can be more safely performed in a hospital, in a room especially adapted for such work. In the single matter of suitable light, for instance, it is easily explained that the surgeon must have light from overhead. No side light from an ordinary window is sufficient to illumine the depths of the incision into the body. And this is only one of the many advantages to both surgeon and patient afforded by the modern hospital, but chief among them all is the already mentioned greater security from blood-poisoning. It would take too long to explain this greater security, and the countless details upon which it depends. Suffice it that the ablest men in the world of science are continually at work upon the subject of disease germs and the means of their eradication. And each hospital strives to adopt in practice the rapid improvements these scientists make known. But these processes of eradicating disease germs are often slow processes, requiring great expenditure of time, money, and attention. It would be as impracticable to provide in the ordinary house for the possible necessity of a surgical operation as it would be to provide a fully equipped machine shop. In short, owing to the rapidly increasing knowledge in the domain of surgery, the difference between a private house and a hospital suitably provided for the safest treatment of patients is a difference of increasing consequence, and even now of almost insurmountable importance.

Owing to the general intelligence and to the increasing interest in such matters, it is not surprising that the hospital movement claims the attention of every progressive community. Almost the first question that confronts those interested in the movement is that of the size of a community which absolutely requires a hospital, and then the size of the hospital required. The question is a complicated one. The advantages of the smaller hospitals have not yet obtained general recognition. The large hospitals have still the prestige of years of splendid service; they have also the curses of self-satisfaction, of red tape in profusion, of sluggishness in adopting improvements. In them the individuality of the patient is lost sight of, the friends and family can visit him only briefly and at stated hours. The regulations, of necessity, must be very strict. True, on the staff of the large hospitals are the ablest physicians and surgeons of the city and of the State. But in reality the direct immediate care of the patients is in the hands of the "house officers," who are either still students of medicine or at best graduates having no acquired skill in the art of healing.

In the smaller hospitals, on the other hand, there is no prestige, no red tape, no self-satisfaction; instead, there is an immediate, eager readiness to adopt every improved method. Owing to the smaller size there is possible a more home-like arrangement: the patient's individuality is not lost; his friends can more easily visit him; and he is under the care of his own physician or surgeon, who, of course, is not so famous as they of the larger hospital staffs, but who nevertheless will devote his whole attention to his patient, and who would not, even if he could, surrender the care of him to unskilled hands.

Some patients would not be distressed by the wholesale *régime* of the famous large hospital; others would prefer being treated nearer home, within calling distance of their friends, by their own doctors. But aside from this question of preference, it sometimes happens that one's distance from a hospital is a question involving life and death. Where one can at one's leisure canvass the pros and cons of different hospitals, that is one thing; it is quite another in the emergencies where an artery is bleeding in the crushed leg, or where an internal abscess has suddenly developed. Then comes the question, Can one be safely moved to the neighboring little hospital? No longer can the famous large-city hospital be considered.

The gist of the matter is that both large and small have their uses, and both are needed; but inasmuch as the advantages of small hospitals are less widely known, and moreover for the reason that the writer's experience is wholly concerned with the same, the following pages will be found to be devoted to the inception and management of small hospitals in small communities.

As regards the question of how large a town may be, without the absence of a hospital being a reflection upon the enterprise and charity of the community, of course much depends upon the location of the town—

much, also, upon the character of its inhabitants. Thus, as is readily seen, a town far removed from any city or larger town, and itself the centre of still smaller neighboring villages, is in far greater need of a hospital than is an even larger but suburban town within easy reach of the large-city hospitals. Then again, a manufacturing town with a shifting population, where many are especially exposed to accidents, and where few have homes of their own, stands in greater need of a small hospital, where sick strangers can be cared for, and where mangled patients can be taken, than does a rural, peaceful community of equal population, where accidents are few, and where every one has his own home.

In the country one expects to be far removed from hospitals, as well as from schools and fire-engines and police and many other conveniences and safeguards of town life. But in any centre of civilization one naturally looks for all its adjuncts. Schools and markets, however, being in ever present need are rightly looked to first ; and only the more thoughtful and experienced residents will look anxiously towards the foundation of a hospital, which after all is only for occasional service. It is well, therefore, at the outset to consider the various uses for which a small hospital serves.

Some of these uses have been already mentioned. But besides the advantages in cases of important surgical operations, which, in the absence of hospital accommodations, are not often attempted, there are other almost equally important advantages to be thought of.

The health of the community depends largely upon the proper isolation of the sick; and the more we know about the nature of diseases the more true does this become. Some diseases have always been considered contagious and infectious. The list of diseases known to be so is constantly growing; and the continued presence of these preventable diseases is a just cause of reproach in any community. True, it may be from faulty water-supply, or from bad drainage, or from other sanitary defects that the zymotic or germ diseases derive their support; but the real root of the evil will always be found in the improper care of patients suffering from these diseases. For the proper care of the sick implies not only a regard for the patients themselves, but also full precautions against the spread of the disease. It is generally recognized that hospitals are necessary for the proper care of patients suffering with smallpox, or Asiatic cholera, or leprosy. It is not generally recognized that hospital care is also necessary for the proper treatment of many other equally contagious and infectious diseases.

If the scarlet fever, or typhoid fever, or diphtheria patient lives in a large house; if others of the family can be sent away for safety; if trained nurses can be afforded; in short, if the patient's house can be transformed into a temporary hospital, then there would be no particular advantage to the patient or to the safety of others in moving him to a hospital. But where any of these conditions is wanting, the danger to the community is very real. Some cities have so fully realized this danger, and by hospital provisions have so fully guarded against it, that they no longer suffer from epidemics. Occasional cases of these dreadful diseases will doubtless occur for many years to come, but in an intelligent community there should never occur any epidemic. Nor would there, if in every such community there was suitable hospital provision for the prompt and complete isolation of cases as they occur, and provision for the temporary isolation of persons who have been exposed to the contagion, and finally provision for the thorough disinfection of all infected clothing and furniture. These are not visionary statements, but verities based upon actual facts. And yet, so little attention is paid to sanitary matters, that less money is usually granted to hospitals and boards of health for this special purpose of fighting contagious diseases than is granted for the fireworks for public holidays. The direct and the indirect money loss caused by sickness and death is so vastly above the loss caused by fire that it would seem a plain business necessity to provide means of fighting contagious disease as well as fire apparatus. And it is as hopeless to prevent the spread of scarlet fever, for instance, without suitable hospital wards for the isolation of patients, and suitable disinfecting stations, as without fire-engines to confine to its place of origin a fire once started in the thickly settled tenement portions of the town.

If anything can be more forlorn than homesickness, it is sickness away from home. And if any sacred duty equals that of providing for one's own, it is that of providing for the sick stranger within our gates. In these days of easy journeying we have not only the helpless tramp fallen by the wayside to care for, and the servants and the laborers whose only homes, very likely are across the seas, but we have also to think of the larger and larger class of visitors and travelling salesmen and agents, who when well are abundantly able to care for themselves, but when overtaken by sickness or accident in hotels and boarding-houses, or worse yet, in lodgings, where there is no provision for their food, to say nothing of care, or in the stable-lofts and garrets of their employers, who, however willing they may be, simply cannot properly care for their sick servants. Then the first question is, where is the nearest hospital?

In olden times there was no floating population. Servants came from neighboring homes, to which, in case of illness, they could easily be returned. The occasional stranger, if sick, was cared for by the whole community, serving in turn as "night-watchers." Then, in the same way if any one family became especially stricken, the burden was shared. But even then how often did the sickness of one entail the sickness and perhaps death of others of the overburdened family! Times have greatly changed. It is not that hearts have grown cold. Those who formerly so freely spent their strength in nursing their neighbors, now in obedience to the advancing conditions of our civilization, spend their strength and their money in building and in managing hospitals, where all this old-time service to the sick and suffering can be, and is done with far better effect.

Done far better,—that is, so far as the patients are concerned. But how about the counter effect upon the hearts of the well-to-do? Are we to lose from the earth that noblest type of woman, whose spirit was never tired by night after night of watching by some poor suffering neighbor's bedside; who carried no card-case, but who directed her calls where God prompted her loving heart to go? Surely some substitute for this old-time service to the neighbor must be found, or well-meaning men and women will again be asking, Who is my neighbor?

And not the least of the uses of a hospital, founded and supported by a small community, is to be found in the knitting together of the hearts of the men and women and children in a noble service, under the inspiration of the very essence of Christianity.

L'Hôtel Dieu, God's Inn, the hospital used to be called, and is so best called to-day. The word hospital itself carries in it the whole spirit of hospitality; and a most suitable dedicatory inscription over every hospital door would be:

"To God and to the stranger forever."

CHAPTER II.

HOW TO INTEREST THE PUBLIC.—PRELIMINARY MEETINGS.—SELECTION OF COMMITTEES.

THE inauguration of any public improvement depends at first upon the enthusiasm of a very few, and afterwards upon the awakened enthusiasm of the many. There is nowadays on the one hand a growing tendency to leave to the government all undertakings designed for the public good, and on the other hand another tendency to take from public management and give over to the churches' control educational and charitable institutions. So far as the good of the churches is concerned it cannot be doubted that that is strengthened and revivified by the undertakings of any active Christian work. But as regards the greatest good to the community which may come from founding and supporting hospital work, there is no doubt that neither by any one religious denomination nor by the public government, but by the co-operation of all these agencies, and also of individuals, is the best way.

And the problem confronting the few whose attention is first given to the hospital question, whose enthusiasm has been first aroused, is how to enlist the support of every existing agency for good works and of every individual in the place. It is indeed a problem. Different societies and circles and different persons must be approached in different ways. One reason for one, another for another, must be advanced until all the reasons requiring the institution, all the advantages that will follow, are clearly understood by all. So much tact and discretion are required in the would-be promoters that many times it seems as if the whole future of the movement depends upon the chance of who happens first to talk of it. But that is really never true. And those who try their best in this as in every good work must not be discouraged if their own ways fail. Let them rather modify their ways and trust fully to the ultimate success of every good motion. There is no such thing as crop failure for good seed, however long in coming may be the harvest-time.

The one great principle for the guidance of those who seek to establish a hospital is to utilize every existing possible agency, and the second principle is to guard jealously the equal representation of every agency employed. Naturally the churches are thought of first. Now, if the work of arousing general interest in the hospital movement is rightly done, each religious denomination and each parish will forever feel an equal share in it. This desirable result cannot be obtained by letting the Baptists, for instance, take up a collection in aid of the enterprise before ever the Methodists or the Unitarians have heard of the proposal. Nor will it do to ask the aid of the Roman Catholics, as an afterthought, after all the offices in the preliminary organization have been filled with Protestants. Each parish must be fairly treated.

Suppose that the original promoters number three— only they must never let their identity as promoters be known. If the movement is to be a popular movement it must not be handicapped by the appearance of its being Mrs. Jones' or Mr. Brown's blessing thrust upon the community. But, further supposing that these three promoters are really in living earnest, let them on the very same day, if possible, call upon each clergyman and upon several of his most influential parishioners to talk with them about the plan. Not to tell them that everything is already on the high road, but to ask their opinions about the usefulness of the movement, about the probabilities of enlisting all the churches and, incidentally, the non-church-goers. The main thing to be found out in these interviews is the person's name in each religious society most sure to be willing to serve in the preliminary organization of the hospital and most sure to represent well his or her society.

Then these representatives are to be assembled. If any fail to appear, every effort must be made to secure some one in his place.

The only question before this first meeting is that of the desirability and necessity of the proposed hospital. It would of course seem both natural and fitting at this stage to have the opinions of the members of the medical profession. Unfortunately there is too much truth in the trite opinion that doctors seldom agree. A special chapter shall be devoted to that question and to the means of persuading them to pull together. But now, at this early and most critical stage of hospital development, no risks must be run. If there is only one physician in the place, then by all means invite him to the meeting, and listen, to him and then be guided by what he says, if he happens fully to approve of the movement.

It is not a bad plan to arrange for the visit of some one well acquainted with some neighboring hospital in a community of equal size, who can tell the meeting of the difficulties in the way and of the advantages secured by surmounting them. No one at this meeting is to be allowed to throw the cold water of doubt as to how the money needed for the purpose is to be raised. Time enough for that question will be allowed later on. The sole question is whether there is need of a hospital. If there is, if any of the advantages enjoyed by other communities having hospitals, or if any of the recognized disadvantages in not having one so appeals to the judgment of this conference as to impose upon it the moral necessity of at least trying to get one for their own community, then let this judgment be duly recorded. And let this conference immediately organize itself into a temporary board of management of the enterprise. Otherwise let it be dissolved to await the enterprise of succeeding generations. We meantime will go on by the optimistic road with those who believe where there's a will there's a way.

The immediate business before the new hospital promoters is to search out every possible helpful agency, and to ask from each some promise of its support for at least one year. Can each church be persuaded to take up a collection for the hospital on one Sunday of the year? Hospital Sunday is popular where it is once begun. Many give then whose hearts and pockets are touched at no other time.

And then, will the different clubs and social circles take an interest in the work? Will the King's Daughters sew for the hospital? Will the Young Men's Christian Association give the needed carriage-hire for moving the sick, as the associations elsewhere so kindly do? Will the Cross-road Corner's Club promise to give to the hospital the proceeds of their next play or minstrel show? In short, will every one take hold and help on the movement for a new hospital? These are some of the countless questions to be asked by the managers of the movement. And these and other questions must be most discreetly asked. It will never do to have Jenkins ask the Smiths who own the factory if they will support a free bed for the possible use of their operatives. Oh no! Let Jenkins undertake the Knights of Cereus. Let Tompkins ask the Smiths—why, he is hand in glove with them. They will back him every time.

So it is the world over. And it is astonishing how easy it always seems to do anything when you know how to do it. The rub comes when no one does know just how to do it. But discouragements come just to try our hearts—to prove if we are in earnest. And it is no easy task to found a hospital—nor, indeed, to found or support anything else that is worth supporting or founding.

In this particular work of canvassing the town to enlist the support of every organization and of all the citizens, comes the great opportunity for making widely known the expected advantages that will ensue. If the aid of the local papers can be secured, so much the better. But, after all, it is by talking, talking, talking, that general interest in an innovation is obtained. Too much must not be expected from the first encounter with the conservative elements. Some are so constituted that they never can accept a new idea on first hearing. To them time must be given. In the end these very individuals may become the most enthusiastic friends of the movement.

When this preliminary canvass has been thoroughly made, a public meeting should be called, not in any church nor in any one society's abode, but in the most public place. And the call should be so generally given that every man, woman, and child shall feel it to be a personal invitation to be present. The managers of the movement will have to work hard to make this meeting a success. Not only is it necessary to arrange beforehand who shall speak, but also almost what shall be said. There will be provision, of course, for the impromptu speeches of any who wish to speak; but it never works well to trust to such in a public meeting where it is hoped to accomplish anything. And at this meeting it is desirable to secure a vote to establish a hospital, and also the appointment of a committee to carry this vote into effect.

The clergymen and the lawyers always speak easily, and then comes the question how to draw out the physicians. This is just the time to do it. Each should be personally asked to attend and to express his views; and there is no harm in asking one if he will not speak of the advantage of a hospital in the matter of protecting the community from the spread of contagious diseases, nor of asking another if he will not explain to the meeting the advantage in cases of accident and of the graver surgical operations.

The presiding officer of the meeting will be able, if

he has enough tact, to draw from the different speakers in turn what remains to be said in order fully to cover the ground. But it is only fair to help him by giving him, with the list of those who will speak, at least the head-lines of what each has been especially asked to say.

It is comparatively an easy matter to plan for the vote of the meeting to go ahead with the scheme; it is more difficult to arrange for the public authorization of the men and women who are to go ahead. If the board already at work has been well chosen, if every class and society is well represented, perhaps the meeting will entrust the public interests to them. The final work of the provisional board is perhaps the hardest of all, for they must carefully select from their own number and from all others the ones who are best fitted and best able to carry on the work. And it does not follow that those most able to interest others in the new movement will be best able to organize and superintend the work. Perhaps in the canvass just made others will have been discovered who are manifestly better able to execute the scheme, and whose interest in it is equally hearty. However that may be, it is a time for no false modesty, for it is a work in which noble souls may rightly volunteer; nor is it a time for any exhibition of mere personal gratification at being made somewhat conspicuous. The utmost frankness in the preliminary meeting is necessary in order surely to secure the best possible list of nominations for the public meeting to act upon. And it is still of the utmost importance that this list shall be of truly representative persons. Each person to be nominated should be directly asked to serve in case of election; for nothing is more disheartening, as a public meeting is on the point of dissolving, than to have one after another rise to withdraw his name. Such doings are contagious.

It matters not the least what name is given either to the preliminary managers of the movement, or to those elected at the public meeting. Commissioners, trustees, committeemen, or simply managers—whatever they may be called, they have a great work before them. They must form a legal organization. They must collect money. Eventually they will be the ones to build the hospital and to manage its work. Legal, business-like methods must be employed. Some of the board should be good financiers; some should be good housekeepers; some should know about building matters; and, most important of all, some should know what hospitals are and what hospital work means. The medical question is thus brought to the front. And although that is to be discussed later, it is necessary now to point out the desirability of having on the board of managers one or two physicians. So much of the work must otherwise be done in the dark, not only in carrying on the hospital, but even more in planning it. Inasmuch as the hospital is a special field for medical and surgical work, and as the managers will have to decide upon the regulations of that work, there is of course abundant opportunity for jealousy in the appointment of one out of two, or of two out of ten medical practitioners. But it will be found in the end to be far better to have made a selection, the best that can be made, than to have attempted to please all parties by appointing on the board two who will quarrel at every opportunity. Nor need there ever be any trouble from the jealousy or rivalry of those not on the board, if only it is forever plain that no professional advantages accrue to the physicians from their office as managers. At all odds let the best men as well as the best women in the community be nominated and elected to carry out these good intentions. We may now pass on to the work directly before them.

CHAPTER III.

HOSPITAL ORGANIZATION.—THE CORPORATION.— THE BOARD OF MANAGERS.— BY-LAWS.— THE EXECUTIVE COMMITTEE.

A HOSPITAL is not simply a building. Indeed, it would be quite possible for a city to have a fine, well-appointed building, dedicated as a hospital, and yet for that city to be unable to provide hospital care for a wounded wayfarer. And again, it might happen in another city, where there was as yet no fine hospital building, or where perhaps what was the hospital had just been burned down, that hospital care could be given to one or to many needing it.

A hospital is essentially an organization of men and women ready to do hospital work. True, it is almost impossible to conceive of such without some sort of a shelter for the sick and wounded for whom they stand ready to work. But a tent, or a new unused barn, or a vacant house, can always be found in less than a day's search and the accommodations required never fail in coming if the hospital itself, the organization, is alive.

The first work, therefore, before the committee to whom the public has just entrusted the new hospital movement is that of organization. And the chief thing to be thought of is to legally qualify this organization for the acquisition of property bequeathed or given in trust for hospital purposes. The necessary steps differ in different States. Legal advice is thus in immediate demand. If, unfortunately, there is no lawyer on the board, it is not improbable that some lawyer in the town will be very willing to give his best services to the good cause by starting the board aright in this most important process of organizing. There will then be a corporation, with by-laws and with duly elected officers. Inasmuch as the sole purpose of this organization is to be able legally to acquire and to hold property, and as it is necessary that all its meetings should be called according to law, and its proceedings likewise recorded, it really simplifies matters to confine the corporation merely to this function of holding property. And this can be done by entrusting the whole hospital management to a committee, which may be elected annually.

The corporation itself may include any number of citizens. Indeed, it is very well to elect as members all who show their interest in the work and are willing to attend the meetings. The members of the corporation are simply corporators, and the real managers of the hospital must be elected by them. To them the managers must make their annual report of the condition and needs of the hospital and of its past year's work. But beyond selecting the managers, the corporation has nothing more to do with their work, which must be untrammelled.

The duties of the corporation being thus simple, it is an easy matter to arrange its by-laws. Here, for instance, is an example that may perhaps serve as a model:

THE BY-LAWS OF THE CORPORATION OF THE UTOPIA HOSPITAL.

I. The name of this Corporation is THE UTOPIA HOSPITAL.

II. (*a*) Any person may become a member of the corporation who shall be elected by a three-fourths vote at the annual meeting, or at any meeting called for the purpose of electing new members, and who shall signify in writing his or her acceptance of election.

(*b*) Membership of the Corporation shall be forfeited by absence from the meetings of the Corporation for three consecutive years.

III. The officers of the Corporation shall be a President, a Vice-President, a Clerk, a Treasurer, and a board of twelve Managers, who shall be elected by ballot, as follows:

The President, Vice-President, Clerk, and Treasurer shall be elected at the annual meeting; the Managers shall be elected also at the annual meeting—at first, four for a term of three years, four for a term of two years, and four for one year, and thereafter four for a term of three years, and as vacancies occur.

IV. The duties of the officers shall be as follows:

(*a*) The President, and, in his absence, the Vice-President, shall preside at all meetings of the Corporation.

(*b*) The Clerk shall call stated meetings of the Corporation, and extra meetings at the request of any three members, by mailing to each member a notice of the meeting four days previously; he shall duly record all the doings of the Corporation.

(*c*) The Treasurer shall receive and hold all moneys acquired by the Corporation; he shall pay out as ordered by vote of the Corporation or of the Board of Managers, and at the annual meeting he shall present a full financial report.

(*d*) The President and the Clerk shall also serve as auditors of the Treasurer's annual report.

(*e*) The Board of Managers shall have full control of the work of the Hospital, and shall make an annual report thereof to the Corporation.

V. The annual meeting shall be held on the first Monday in January. A majority of the members shall constitute a quorum.

VI. These By-laws may be altered or amended at any meeting; notice of such alterations and amendments having been given at a previous meeting, and also in the Clerk's call of the meeting.

After these by-laws or any others have been adopted, it is proper for all members of the committee appointed at the public hospital meeting to sign the same. The organization has then become a reality, and the corporation is ready to elect its officers. This done, the corporation is free to undertake any work by committees appointed for special purposes, or by acting together. Thus, for instance, if it is desirable to hunt for the best location of the hoped for hospital, or to interview the town officials to find out if public lands or public funds may be had, special committees may well act for the corporation. But if, on the other hand, a complete canvass of the community for funds is voted to be first in order, then the corporation may well act as a whole, each member taking his share of territory to cover.

One of the services that can be well rendered by the members of the corporation, after a hospital is established, is that of making regular visits of inspection, and of reporting to the managers any criticisms or suggestions for improvement. It would be a good plan for the president of the corporation, at the annual meeting, to appoint a list of visitors to the hospital, two for each month in the year.

Meanwhile, if the managers idly wait for a building, or for a goodly bank-account in the treasurer's hands, before getting all ready to begin hospital work, they will make a great mistake.

Kindly disposed testators will not be so likely to leave generous slices of their estates to a corporation whose officers are unprepared to use even what they have. Nor is it a simple task before them, this getting ready for work. Their first business is to adopt by-laws. The corporation entrusts to them the whole control of the hospital's work. It is for them to decide upon all questions of general policy, to engage the officers who are to have direct charge of the execution of their orders, and to adopt such rules and regulations as will ensure the orderly progress of the work.

Before adopting their by-laws it would thus seem necessary that the managers should have definitely decided just how to carry on their work. This would certainly require of them the possession both of vivid imaginations and of a remarkable unanimity, were it not for the help at hand in the published experience of other similar institutions. It is easy to secure the annual reports of all the small hospitals in the State, or in the country for that matter; and not much study of the by-laws of other hospitals is needed in order to throw great light upon the whole question.

It will be quickly seen that the underlying principle of all such organization is that of the division of labor. An army differs from a mob simply in the fact that in the army each man knows exactly what is expected of him. He knows his place so well that he can find it and keep in it the darkest of nights. Each officer knows the extent of his responsibility. So it is on shipboard; each has his duty and does it. So must it be in a hospital. Discipline is as necessary there as in a fort or aboard a man-of-war; and it is equally necessary in a hospital to have one person in supreme command.

In large hospitals this commander is the superintendent. In small hospitals the matron usually holds the reins. Now it is her duty to manage the hospital according to the managers' orders. The by-laws of the managers must therefore either contain their orders for the management of the hospital, or these orders must be published separately under the title of "Rules and Regulations of the Utopia Hospital."

The latter seems to be the simpler way. And then the by-laws of the managers need only cover their own work. The board must have a president and secretary, whose duties shall be such as usually pertain to their offices. And then, in obedience to this foundation principle of all effective organization, the board should resolve itself into separate committees, which shall each attend to one particular part of the management. Thus there should be one committee on strictly medical matters, another committee on housekeeping, another on accounts and reports, and another on the nursing-service, and perhaps other committees on other branches of the work. Three is a good number to have on a small working committee.

In this way each manager will have some particular duty in planning the orders that will be given out by the whole board and in superintending the execution of these orders. But different interests are very liable to conflict with each other, and unless some provision is made for the harmonious working of these committees there might result no end of confusion. Each committee should have its chairman, who can act for the committee at that committee's pleasure. And these chairmen of the various committees ought to meet frequently, as an executive committee of the managers, charged with the duty of acting for the board when not in session.

Such are the main features needed in the by-laws,

and the following draft will make these features plainer :

THE BY-LAWS OF THE MANAGERS OF THE UTOPIA HOSPITAL.

I. The officers of this Board shall be a President and Secretary, who shall be elected at the first meeting after the annual meeting of the Corporation, and whose duties shall be such as usually pertain to their offices.

II. The Managers shall meet on the first Wednesday in each month, and at other times at the request of any two members.

III. Standing committees, of three members each, on Accounts and Reports, on Medical Matters, on Housekeeping, and on Nursing-service shall be elected by ballot at the first regular meeting after the annual meeting of the Corporation, the member receiving the highest number of votes being thus elected to the chairmanship of those committees. In case of two or more members receiving the same number of votes, another ballot shall be taken to decide the chairmanship.

IV. The chairmen of the standing committees, together with the President of the Managers (who shall here serve as chairman), shall constitute the Executive Committee of the Board of Managers.

V. The Executive Committee shall act for the Managers in the intervals of the Managers' meetings, and shall fully report to them at each meeting.

VI. These By-laws may be altered or amended at any regular meeting, or at any meeting called for the purpose, by a three-fourths vote of all the Managers.

Having adopted their by-laws, and having elected their officers and committees, the managers are ready for real work. If a railroad accident occurs that night and the question comes flashing over the wires to Utopia asking if the new hospital is ready to receive a dozen mangled patients, the answer can be made in the affirmative. The executive committee can be assembled, each member will have some definite part of the task already assigned him, and an improvised hospital will be ready on the arrival of the train bearing the wounded.

We will hope, however, that no such exigency will happen, but, instead, that ample time will be had to draw up carefully the rules and regulations by which the hospital is to be governed, to purchase and prepare all sorts of hospital material for the comfort and relief of the suffering, and otherwise to carry into good effect all the good intentions of the Utopia Hospital managers.

CHAPTER IV.

THE MEDICAL QUESTION.— HOMŒOPATHY AND ALLOPATHY.— A POSSIBLE SOLUTION OF THE DIFFICULTY.—THE SELECTION OF THE STAFF. —CHARGES FOR PROFESSIONAL SERVICES TO HOSPITAL PATIENTS.

THE medical question is the bugbear of hospital management. As the reader will have noticed, it has been possible to dodge it thus far only by promising to devote a separate chapter to its consideration.

So many opposing interests are involved, and so much of the opposition is beyond the comprehension of laymen who have never given special attention to the question, that it is no wonder the managers of new hospitals so often stumble over it.

It is in itself a very difficult question ; but there is hope for its final and satisfactory solution in any community where the question itself is fairly stated and the essential difficulty generally understood. Thus it is no exception to the rule that any problem, if truthfully stated, is already more than half solved.

The medical question that confronts hospital managers is, however, not a simple one. It is really a combination of questions, which must be sifted down, till each can be separately considered, before any solution is possible. Some of the separate questions that contribute to the general difficulty are very apparent, and indeed unduly prominent, while others are not easily unmasked.

The chief difficulty concerns the so-called different schools. In common parlance and in common belief there are at present in this country two schools of medical practice—one the old school or allopathic, and the other the homœopathic or new school. There are also other schools,—the eclectic or Thompsonian, for instance,—and there have more lately arisen schools of Faith-cure, Mind-cure, and of Christian Science healing. But hospitals are not likely to be vexed by any question concerning these smaller schools. The real difficulty comes in what may be called the homœopathic question.

The first surprise in store for investigators into this question is the wrathy repudiation by all physicians of the term "allopath." The homœopathists cherish a theory of cure which is expressed by the word "homœopathy." So they, naturally enough, are willing to be called by that name. But physicians who do not happen to believe in any theory of cure naturally object to the name "allopath," which implies a belief, or a theory of practice, never countenanced if indeed it ever existed. The early homœopathists called all others allopathists. That was and is considered a reproach by all who know what the word means. And that is why the designation is so indignantly repudiated by the ordinary physician.

When it comes to the terms "old school" and "new school," there again is found an unwillingness on the part of every physician to be called of the old school. The whole science of medicine, while as old as Galen, is still so rapidly improving that no member of the profession likes to be thought possessed of only time-honored methods.

Thus as the question is studied the difficulty increases of finding acceptable terms in which to describe the very evident differences that divide the medical profession. Well may the managers ask, in despair, of the men who will not be called allopaths or old-school doctors, "What will you allow yourselves to be called?" Unfortunately the answer will not be very satisfactory, the reason being that the great majority of physicians disclaim any particular system of practice. They feel themselves free to use any remedy or to adopt any methods or measures that promise relief to their patients; and so they want to be free from any prefix to their simple title of doctor of medicine, given them by their universities. They want to be called simply physicians or surgeons, just as lawyers are called attorneys or counsellors at law. But this wish of most doctors not to have any extra designation, it must be allowed, is very inconvenient. And the public is so wedded to the use of the names "old school," and "allopath," and "regular," and the names are now used in such entire ignorance of the doctors' antipathy to them, that it is only on such occasions as that of a hospital's advent that vehement protests are evoked. No wonder the new managers are astonished at the outburst.

And still, in spite of the inconvenience in not having a handy name for the medical practitioners in the community who are not homœopathists, it is perhaps not too much to ask of the managers that they shall respect the wishes of the common doctors in this matter, and speak of them simply as physicians and surgeons. This much is sure: by accepting the inconvenience and gratifying them in this matter, much will have been accomplished towards a satisfactory solution of the main question.

Strange as it may at first appear, it is nevertheless true that most of the bitterness attached to the question will be found among the laity and not among the doctors. Indeed, the different kinds of doctors generally pull fairly well together. They visit in the same families; they are always willing to help each other in emergencies; and often they are very good friends. In some localities they consult together, but this is not generally the case.

Now, in almost every community large enough to have a hospital, there are many homœopathists. Even if there is not a physician of that school, there are many families who believe in homœopathic practice, and at any time a homœopathic practitioner may settle there. In large cities the homœopathists have their own hospitals. But in smaller communities that is, of course, impracticable; and it is only fair that, in the small hospital founded and supported by the public, the homœopathists should have equal rights and privileges.

Many different plans have been adopted to accomplish this desirable condition. In some hospitals there are two distinct staffs. Patients desiring homœopathic treatment are referred to the homœopathic staff, and patients who have no choice are alternately likewise referred. But this is a particularly objectionable plan, for it perpetuates and emphasizes the differences and dissensions which all desire to have lessened and ended. There is in this plan, too, an essential absurdity, which rightly brings upon all concerned the ridicule, if not the contempt, of their fellow-practitioners. The absurdity is in asking patients to state the kind of practice they will have—patients who, very likely, not only have no choice, but who are in blissful ignorance of the existence of schools and methods and systems of medical practice. The chief objection to this plan, however, is that by accepting it every physician and surgeon admits the existence of two schools, and moreover assents to the fact of his belonging to one or other of them. As has been already said, the homœopathist very properly can do this; but the physician who does not hold to any particular theory and system of practice cannot do it except at the expense of principle. And in fact, so far as the writer is informed, those who have accepted this arrangement justify their acceptance only by the cheapening excuse of expediency. It is true that where this plan has been adopted the management has tried to make it as acceptable as possible by describing the different staffs as members of this or of that medical society. This thinly hides the underlying objections; and in fact at such hospitals the question put to the incoming patient, who perhaps can neither read nor write his name, is, "Do you wish for homœopathic or allopathic treatment?" And although to casual view such hospitals seem to flourish, yet the best practitioners will not be found there; nor will the work be exemplary. To sum up the advantages and disadvantages of this double-staff plan in a single sentence, it may be said that it apparently is a fair plan for all, but it does not meet the conscientious approval of physicians and surgeons who hold to no one theory of practice; it does not secure for hospital service the best fitted therefor; and, inasmuch as it is essentially a compromise, which hides the real question at issue, it cannot really succeed.

Fortunately there are other plans for us to consider. One is to avoid in the by-laws and in the rules and regulations of the management all reference to the existence of different methods of practice, and to allow to every patient the right to choose his own physician. If the patient has no choice, then he is put under the charge of the number of the staff happening at that time to be on duty.

Now, if homœopathic practitioners were elected to positions upon this staff, this plan would be an ideal one. And presumably any homœopathic practitioner, if elected as a homœopathist, would be willing to serve the hospital in this capacity. But this difficulty at once presents itself: most practitioners who obstinately refuse to be especially designated will not serve on a staff or on a medical board where any are elected as representatives of a particular school.

This seems at first sight only an instance of pig-headedness; but on further examination it will appear not unreasonable, and furthermore that we are nearing the very root of the difficulty.

Why is it, then, that the doctors who are on such friendly terms with their homœopathic brethren in every-day life will not serve with them on a hospital staff? They go to the same private family, one to one patient, the other to the other. In emergencies they will give each other aid. Why cannot they, in the same way, serve the hospital? The homœopathist is willing; the other is not.

The reason of his refusal is that he cannot accept a position on a board or staff where the existence of one school of medicine is recognized, without thereby abetting the already extensive popular error that he himself belongs to a school, and is bound to one particular theory or system of medical practice. This is the whole truth of the matter. His refusal is not based upon prejudice, nor upon jealousy, nor upon simple obstinacy, but upon conscientious principles, which he is ever hoping may become more generally understood.

Granting for the time that his principles are flimsy and doomed to eventual sacrifice, is it not possible for the Utopia Hospital to respect the positions and the desires of both parties to this question. Would not the following plan accomplish this:

First, let every patient choose his own physician, and the hospital in behalf of that patient ask the favor of that physician's services.

Second, let the hospital ask the physicians in the community to inform the hospital during what portions of the year they will be ready to respond to such calls, and also to give their regular attendance. Then let the managers elect from the volunteers a staff to serve by turns for a year; and in this election let the fitness of the practitioners as physicians and surgeons be the sole guidance to the managers. And let there be no mention of schools.

Third, in order to ensure perfect fairness to the homœopathists and to the patients who may desire that form of treatment, let the managers arrange for the constant appointment of a homœopathic practitioner, or of a set of them as homœopathic specialists to the hospital.

If the Utopia Hospital managers will adopt this plan they will find it to possess these merits: Patients of the hospital will have the greatest possible freedom in choosing their professional attendants, the poorest beggar being in this respect as rich as the Crœsus of the city. The principles and wishes of the so-called old-school regulars will be respected, and their hearty coöperation will be assumed. And, finally, the homœopathic physicians will have the double privilege: first, of serving on the regular staff undesignated except by the honor of success in an open election at the hands of their fellow-citizens; and, second, of serving as homœopathic specialists, and of being so designated.

This homœopathic question, although so prominent, is by no means the most important division of our subject. That is rather the problem of securing the best medical and surgical talent, regardless of all else. In hospitals where patients have no choice in the matter of their medical attendants, the positions on the staff carry far greater prestige; but still, in however small a hospital, an appointment to the staff is an honor. And, although where free choice of attendants is allowed the patients, much less devolves upon the staff surgeons, yet the responsibility upon the management is no less to furnish the best possible surgical attention to the poor, mangled brakeman who is brought to the hospital unconscious, and unable to choose his surgeon even if he knew any in the place.

This responsibility must not be shirked. The managers must not yield to the temptation to elect Dr.

Smith because of his supposed influence with the large donors to the hospital, if they are satisfied that some other surgeon of less influence among the wealthy is really better fitted for the position. Nor may the managers decide in favor of one on the grounds of personal friendship. If they do so mistake their duty they make themselves in part responsible for the sufferings and deaths in the hospital which might have been prevented by a better surgeon.

But, it may be urged by a timorous manager, How can a lay board judge as to the merits of the different surgeons available? At the start this is not an easy matter. After the hospital work has begun it is easy to find out who give most attention to their patients, who comply most scrupulously with all of the hospital regulations, and who really stand first in the estimation of their professional brethren. And even before this test of experience, in the conferences which the managers will have had with all of the members of the medical profession they will become enabled to judge fairly well who the ablest are, and who will be most likely to give the hospital their very best service.

As a general rule the younger members of the profession are able to do most for the hospital. They are likely to be more acquainted with modern hospital methods, and to have more time to devote to hospital work; they have their reputations still to make—they must do well.

It need not, however, be supposed that all the vexations of the medical question are ended with the election of the staff. Countless matters will be coming up which would sorely vex the managers did that board not have a committee on medical matters to which all such questions may be referred. Only the large questions of policy need to be discussed in the full meetings; the details can be well left to the medical committee.

One of the questions that will come before the full board is that of professional fees for services rendered to patients in the hospital. It is a question that has been discussed for ages. In some hospitals no fees are allowed to be charged under any circumstances. In others it is the customary and expected thing for the professional attendants to charge and to be paid for their services. Still again in other hospitals the surgeons are allowed to charge their fees, except during their own particular months of service, when they are expected to serve gratuitously.

There are many sides to the question. On one view it would seem that the surgeons and physicians are paid for their work, indirectly, by the prestige of their connection with the hospital. To those who look at it in this way it no doubt seems that all medical fees are in a measure extortions. But, from another point of view, doctors are seen to do a deal of gratuitous work. And in the hospital itself, for the charity patients, they cheerfully do their best, without thought of money recompense. Why should they attend gratuitously patients in the hospital, who are able to pay for all they receive, and who would of course pay for medical attendance at their own homes?

The tradesmen charge for supplying food to the hospital patients, whether paying or free patients; the druggists charge for their medicines. Why, then, should not the doctor, who charges nothing for attending the poor, charge those who can pay him?

Take, for instance, the case of a fairly wealthy man who breaks his leg and is taken to the hospital; or one similarly well off, in whom there develops the need of some surgical operation, and who goes to the hospital. Each there, in paying the hospital charges, will pay out far less than equal attention would have cost him at home. Why should either be relieved of paying the proper charges for his surgical attendance?

So far as the recipients of the hospital's charity are concerned, there is of course no question. For them all professional attendance is entirely gratuitous. And then there is another class of patients just able to pay the regular hospital charges, but not able to pay more. One reason why they go to the hospital is to be relieved of every avoidable expense. The needs of this class can be met by the provision of gratuitous attendance by members of the staff serving in rotation.

Another class of patients, who also cannot pay more than the hospital charges, and who nevertheless especially want the services of some particular surgeon, can be provided for by allowing such the privilege of requesting any they please, and making with him their own terms.

Then those who can pay for their professional attendance, and who from the hospital as from their own homes, or from a hotel, send for their family doctor, or for some other physician or surgeon, may be fairly expected to pay the usual charges for what they thus receive.

The one drawback to this great freedom of choice allowed to all patients is the variety and number of doctors that will be in attendance at the same time. This bothers the nurses, and leads to more or less confusion. But, after all, it is the best way yet devised for meeting fairly all the needs and interests which it is incumbent upon a small hospital to serve.

For the protection of the hospital, and for the good order of the work, it is necessary to require of every physician and surgeon attending patients in the hospital to write out each day, in books provided for the purpose, both his reports of the cases and his orders for the coming day. It is also necessary to require daily visits from all having patients in the hospital under their charge.

CHAPTER V.

THE NURSING SERVICE.—ESTABLISHING A TRAINING-SCHOOL.—SELECTION OF A SUPERINTENDENT.—PROBATIONERS AND STUDENT NURSES.

MUCH as the success of a hospital depends upon its medical and surgical staff, even more does it depend upon its nursing service. No matter how well the orders are given, all depends upon their good execution.

There are three ways of providing the nursing service in a small hospital. The first way is by hiring nurses who have been trained elsewhere. The chief disadvantage of this plan is its expensiveness. Trained nurses can earn such high wages in private nursing that they cannot afford, except at high rates, to take permanent positions where they will have no special opportunities for rising in their profession. And in a small hospital there are no such opportunities. Much of the nursing service is necessarily monotonous. It is no wonder that nurses who have already received their training do not like to do the work that might just as well be done in great part by untrained nurses.

The advantage of this first plan, if the hospital can afford it, is that the management is entirely relieved of all vexations as to the nursing service. The work will be well done. All that is needed is a capable matron, who can keep the reins well in hand. A set of trained nurses is a strong team.

The second plan is a modification of the first. By hiring besides the matron, who herself is a trained nurse, as many other trained nurses as are needed to fill the positions of head-nurses, and then by hiring young women of the upper-servant class, who can be taught to do the main part of the work under the constant superintendence of the head-nurses, the patients can be very well cared for. Such girls can be hired at a little above servants' wages; and, although more nurses will be needed, yet the total cost will be less than by the first plan. Where untrained help can be readily obtained, this plan works well. The girls soon learn to do the ordinary work very well, and in emergencies there are several trained nurses to call upon. The chief disadvantage is that the nursing-work is done simply for weekly wages, and by girls who have no inducement to give better and better service. After all, such nurses are servants, and the hospital loses the services of the ambitious, capable young women who clamor for admission to those hospitals that have regular training-schools.

The third, and by far the best, plan is for every hospital, however small, to have its nursing service done by the student nurses of a training-school. Such service costs far less than the other kinds. Moreover, in this way is secured the service of the finest women in the land; for training-schools now receive as students only well-educated, refined, young women, who by nature are already well fitted to enter this noble profession.

But how, it may be asked, is the new hospital to secure such advantages, when there is as yet no training-school within perhaps hundreds of miles? If there is no other way, let the hospital start a training-school. Indeed, this is the usual process. Sometimes, however, training-schools are first started, and hospitals afterwards as adjuncts. But this is not the best way. Nor is it advisable for the hospital to take upon itself the management of a training-school, unless there is no other way. It is far better for some of the managers, with any others who may likewise be especially interested in the subject of training nurses, to undertake this work independently. Then the training-school can furnish nurses to the hospital. And this can be done at low rates, in return for the advantage thereby gained for the school in the opportunity for instruction.

Were hospital wards the only places where nurses can be trained, there would not be any great gain in delegating the business to any outside institution. And many, who have had experience only with the large hospital training-schools, still believe that this is the fact. But it is not so. And even the best of the large hospital training-schools are now beginning to recognize this, and, for the purpose of increasing the efficiency of their graduate nurses, are now planning for portions of their studentship outside the hospital walls.

The great advantages, both to the medical profession and to those in need of nursing service, furnished by training-schools which send out their student nurses to private service, need not be more than mentioned

here. I have elsewhere fully discussed the subject.*
But it is necessary here to show how feasible it is for
such an auxiliary association to furnish at extremely
low rates the nursing service of a small hospital. For
on account of the dependence of hospital work upon
efficient nursing service, such provision becomes almost
the first duty of the hospital managers.

The ease with which trained nurses can now be
secured, who are fully competent to superintend a
hospital, and also to carry on a training-school wherein
others can be likewise trained, has already been mentioned as one of the causes of the new hospital movement. Such a woman, being able to superintend both
the small hospital and the training-school, allows a
saving of hospital money, because her salary can properly be divided between the two institutions that she
serves. Thus a considerable economy is effected.

From the very nature of its work, which must always be largely charitable, a hospital depends for its
support upon either private endowments and subscriptions, or else upon the public purse. But a properly
managed training-school, on the other hand, should be
fully self-supporting; and that, too, while furnishing
nursing service at low rates to its sister institution, the
hospital, and also, at no cost whatever, the charity
nursing needed in the community. All that is needed
in order to establish this desirable condition of things
is a small income for the use of the training-school
during its first year, until it is fairly inaugurated.

This makes plain some of the reasons why it is better to have the two institutions separate. The train-

---

* Training-Schools for Nurses in Small Cities. Geo. E. Ellis: Boston.

ing-school can easily earn its own way; and general knowledge of that fact, unless the training-school is plainly a separate institution, seriously hampers all efforts to secure contributions for the hospital. Then, again, as every such institution obtains, and probably in part fairly deserves, more or less criticism and opposition in the field of its operations, it is only a wise precaution not to let that apply also to the hospital. The training-school, being independent of public support, is far better able to bear single-handed all censure and dissatisfaction than the hospital is able to bear even a part of it.

There is nothing miraculous in the financial success of a training-school for nurses. In other kinds of training-schools no profit is expected from the work produced. But in this the students are taught while in actual service, for which the school charges and receives due money compensation; meanwhile, the student nurses are paid for their labor by the instruction given them. Nor are the instructors paid from the school's treasury. They are paid by the advantages they have in any desired amount of nursing service for their families and friends and charity patients, and by the great conveniences they thus obtain in their work.

There are of course some necessary expenses in carrying on such a school. There is the salary of the superintendent, which, as has just been said, may well be divided with the hospital—at least at first, when both institutions are in their early stages. And then a small monthly money allowance must be given to the student nurses for incidental expenses; and they must also be boarded by the school when not out at private service or assigned to hospital work. It is necessary, therefore, to have some home for them, which serves also as headquarters, where they report each afternoon for instruction and for their orders. Then there are other minor expenses—for the laundry, for books and stationery; for telephone communication with the hospital, the doctors, and the families desiring nurses; and for countless other incidentals. But all these expenses can be met by the income earned by the student nurses in service where the patients are able and willing to pay for it.

As would be naturally inferred, it is far easier to start a training-school for nurses than it is to start a hospital. And it is equally plain that no greater help can be given to the new hospital movement than can be given by inaugurating a training-school. The latter naturally leads to the former. So ready is the training-school, when in running order, to do real hospital work that, unless the hospital managers bestir themselves to carry their plans into effect, the training-school will soon be having a hospital of its own.

For, in nursing the sick poor, it will immediately be very plain that much better work could be done, and at great saving of expense, by removing the patients from their wretched surroundings to some central and more sanitary quarters. If this is done a temporary hospital is the result. But then the training-school, instead of being concerned only with the nursing of these patients, which is quite enough, would have to assume also the expenses and the general management of the affair; whereas, it is just for this work that the hospital organization has been created.

No better illustration could be given of the mutual dependence of the two institutions. And this is assuredly the fitting time to urge those who are especially interested in the subject of the training-school for nurses to begin their labors. All interested in the new hospital will wish them God-speed.

There are many advantages and no disadvantages in having some of the hospital managers also directors of the training-school. The interests of both are thus served; and their interests are largely identical.

The committee of the hospital managers on nursing-service surely ought to be ready to take active part in the organization of the training-school. So ought all the members of the hospital staff. Perhaps some other physicians in the community may be found who will also be eager to join in the work, and who, during their own previous residence in other hospitals, have taken part in the training of the nurses there. And then outside of the board of managers, among the corporators, or even outside of all who have shown any interest in the hospital movement, may also be found women who will gladly aid in the work.

The few who are especially interested should carefully select, from all available persons, perhaps a dozen who may be expected to give most valuable aid. It is not necessary to canvass the town, nor to hold any public meetings in starting this work; for it is not to be dependent upon public support. It is, however, necessary at the outset to obtain a few hundred dollars, and also a guaranty of as much more, to fall back upon, in case of need during the first year. And this ought to be no difficult matter; for it can be truthfully stated, in soliciting this money, that every penny received will eventually be used in furnishing nursing service to those who need it and could never pay for it.

In many cities there are district-visiting nurse societies, which annually secure large contributions for this work of charity nursing. And therefore those who can give may very properly be asked for the little money, and for the small guaranty, that is needed to institute the training-school, which will at once and for all time undertake this most needed charity.

In asking for even this it is only fair, as far as possible, not to interfere with the canvass which very likely is being made simultaneously for the hospital. Some do not like to be asked for money, even for charity, twice in the same day. On the other hand, those who give most freely of their time and of their money are the very ones who, when giving, thank those who present to them the opportunities.

Having obtained the necessary funds and guaranty, the promoters of the training-school may immediately organize. It does not matter much what by-laws they adopt. They need a name; and for officers a president, clerk, and treasurer; and there is need also of a small executive committee to act for the whole board, when it is not in session, and in matters too unimportant to demand assembling it. The officers of the board may well constitute this committee.

Then they must all study up the subject. Books, more interesting than novels, may now be had which tell about nurse-heroines and about famous schools; and others, only less interesting, which tell of the details of management in these institutions. Some of the directors of the new school possibly can spare the time to visit the schools already in operation, and, if not, to collect by correspondence all that can be had of the reports, the rules and regulations, and the printed "blanks" used by these schools in their work.

The first real business for the directors is to secure the right woman for superintendent. And as the hospital is at least equally interested in this matter, a conference committee must take it in charge. And, as this is only the first of a never-ending series of questions, where both the hospital and the training-school will be equally interested, it will be well to arrange for the permanence of this joint committee.

By applying to other training-schools, any number of candidates for the position of superintendent can be secured. Every school appreciates the compliment of being thus asked to nominate a candidate. Each, naturally enough, enjoys in anticipation the extension of its own methods, by the natural increase of nurses who will inevitably bear more or less resemblance to the ancestral stock.

In the embarrassment of opportunities thus showered upon the committee entrusted with the selection of one upon whose ability and natural fitness for the work so much will depend, it is not unwise to be guided by the characteristics of the ancestral stock. In general, it may be truly said that a nurse whose only training has been in a large hospital will not be so able as one from a smaller school to manage a small institution. Some knowledge of wholesale trade may, however, enhance the worth of a retail clerk. And if a nurse can be found who is thoroughly acquainted with the work of both large and small hospitals, so much the better. But for the training-school work it is absolutely necessary that, either in her studentship or afterwards in a special course there, she should have acquired a perfect understanding of the methods of training in the schools where much of the training is given outside the hospital walls.

Having secured a suitable superintendent, the directors can rest awhile upon their oars. She will be able to present to them a scheme for the new school, which, if necessary, they can help her to modify, in order to make it better fit the locality of Utopia.

There will doubtless be some friction at first, due to misunderstanding of the respective responsibilities of the directors and of the superintendent. The work is new. The superintendent will have her own very positive ideas as to how it shall be carried on. And, while willing enough to carry out the policy adopted by the directors and plainly expressed to her, she will not relish any interference with the details of her management. She may rightly ask for written instructions, in order that there may never be any question as to the orders which she is expected to execute. She is responsible for the work of her nurses; therefore, she should be the one to select them, and to discharge them, if need be. In this, as in all her work, she acts subject to the approval of the board of directors; but in every way her authority as captain must be maintained.

After a general scheme for the school has been adopted, applications for admission may be considered. Although the superintendent should be held responsible for the selection of her nurses, after she has had a chance to try them, it may be necessary at first for the directors to take some steps to secure likely " probationers." Again, by communicating with other schools already famous, names can be secured of applicants there who, rather than wait their turn of admission, would like to enter a new school.

In selecting probationers the one great question is whether to give preference to applicants who live near by. On the whole, it is better, at least at first, to take others. At any rate, it is not well to let the item of local residence weigh in their favor. For while nurses, after they have received their training, are likely to succeed exceptionally well in their own communities, yet, while in process of training, it is better for them to be well away from their friends and acquaintances. But questions of race, of religious denomination, of locality of present and former homes, count as nothing in comparison with the questions of their health and strength and natural fitness for the work. There need be no doubt that plenty will apply, and no matter what delay, let no second best be taken even as probationers.

Very soon the school will be in operation. The doctors will be giving their daily lessons, and taking the student nurses out to help them in their work, perhaps to leave them as night-watchers. And in cases where skilled nursing is not required, or cannot be afforded, the student nurses will be doing their best. At such places they will be cheered on by the doctors, who will prolong their visits to tell them just what to do and how to do it. The superintendent will also make them a morning call, to criticise their work, and to show them how to bring about that comfortable tidiness that only skill and training can effect.

Each afternoon the student nurses will come back to the home to hear the lecture, and to get, with their cup of refreshing tea, renewed inspiration for the weary watches before them. Soon they will be bringing back to the amazed directors all sorts of compliments for the training-school.

And the directors may soon confidently offer to the hospital managers all the nursing service desired.

CHAPTER VI.

THE TEMPORARY HOSPITAL.—TRANSFORMATION OF DWELLING-HOUSE. — TEMPORARY NEW WARDS.—COTTAGE WARD FOR CONTAGIOUS DISEASES.—FURNISHINGS.—THE AMBULANCE.

EVERY workman must have his workshop. Without it, by carrying his tools to different houses, he can get along for a time; but unless he has his own shop, with its bench and other fittings, he will not be able to do his best work.

So is it with a hospital organization that is ready for work, and yet has no place to do it in. By taking advantage of the help the training-school for nurses stands ready to give, and by sending one or other of the staff surgeons out to needing patients; by sending out also food and clothing and medicines, the hospital organization can do something towards fulfilling its mission. But its real work is begun only when it has opened the doors of some home of its own for the entrance of the afflicted. Any home will do for this real beginning. A tent will do in summer, or in the far South during any season. A common dwelling-house often suffices for a hospital's first years.

The building of a permanent hospital ought to be very slowly undertaken, and never hurried at the expense of the best possible workmanship. In this country building almost always is too hurried. Few here, even of the costly hospitals, can fairly be expected to outlast some in Europe which already are centuries old. And yet not only the permanence but the quality of the hospital, in the vital matter of its freedom from contamination, is jeopardized by too hurried building.

And, again, it is a matter requiring long thought and study to get the best possible plans for a hospital. Especially is this so when those who are to decide upon the merits of various plans know little as yet about other hospitals, or, indeed, about the work of the hospital which they must house. So much must be said about the permanent hospital, that the subject may well be postponed for a subsequent chapter.

But it will not do for the hospital organization, before beginning its real work, to wait for a permanent home. For, should this be done, several misfortunes would result. The hospital buildings would not be exactly fitted for the work, as nobody could know beforehand just what the work would require. And then inevitably the work of building would be hurt by being hurried in response to the outcry for the hospital work to begin. And still, worst of all, the delay in beginning hospital work would allow a fading out of the popular eagerness for it, and willingness to support it.

On the other hand, if some temporary hospital buildings are utilized, the public interest will have some object upon which it can be concentrated and where it can be fostered: the managers will have not only plenty of time for building well the permanent hospital, but they will also have time for becoming acquainted with their work—they can grow with it.

Some objection may be felt to beginning the work in anything short of a fine building. Such objections are not well grounded. As reasonable would it be for a religious society to wait for its permanent church edifice before beginning to hold its services: unless the church's work be begun in a log house, or, even before that, under the shelter of the forest's natural arches, would not that church forfeit its right to exist? Can any other fate be fit for a hospital organization that idly waits for the slow growth of walls of brick and stone?

In time of need, the home of any well-to-do patient, at twenty-four hours' notice, can be turned into a fairly good hospital. If it be an old-fashioned house, with open fireplaces, and yet having some of the modern improvements, such as a furnace and good plumbing arrangements, it will be quite easy to make a comfortable hospital of it. And if such a house can be obtained some months before it is needed for a hospital, it can at a moderate expense be made very suitable. Or if an ordinary dwelling-house, suitably located, with plenty of vacant land around it, can be secured, then on this vacant land temporary hospital wards can be quickly built, and at small expense. By connecting these wards with the house by means of corridors a hospital is obtained of most modern and approved plan.

When the permanent hospital is ready these temporary wards can be sold as sheds, or even as kindling-wood; and the cost of them distributed over several years will be less than the rent of other accommodations. The original house would be just as good as before.

The expense of carrying out either of these plans depends of course upon the locality, upon the prices of houses and land, and of building material. Unfortunately little help can be gained by studying other hospital reports, so different are all these conditions in different parts of the country.

The objects to be gained, however, are the same the world over. In the first place, then, let us consider what is most desirable in the situation of a hospital. It is not time yet to choose the best location. Let the building committee find that for the permanent hospital. For these temporary quarters it is necessary to find a building as well as a site. The choice, moreover, is limited by the necessity of having the hospital not too far from the centre of the town. It must be in an accessible place, and yet sufficiently retired to be out of the noise and dust of the busiest places.

For the convenience and advantage of both institutions the hospital and the home of the training-school for nurses must be very near neighbors. There will thus be saved to the hospital the necessity of providing living rooms and chambers for the nurses employed there, and also all the trouble of boarding them. To a small hospital just starting this is a great saving. And as the requirements in the matter of situation are practically the same for both institutions, there ought to be no difficulty in effecting this proximity.

If possible, the situation must be above the general level in order to insure good air and good drainage. Finally, the water-supply must be the very best that can be had in that portion of the country.

So much for the matter of location. And now let us consider first what must be done to transform a common house into a hospital. Afterwards we can take up the rather more attractive subject of building temporary hospital wards to be connected with an ordinary house.

For economy's sake no alterations not absolutely necessary must be made which would leave the house in more unsalable condition when the hospital moves to its permanent abode. Some of the alterations advisable may indeed increase the worth of the building.

The cellar is first to be looked to. If the house is an old one the cellar will be found too low. But it is not much of a job to raise a frame house a few feet on jack-screws and to build under it a higher underpinning. True the chimneys are heavy; but even so the screws will lift them, and their foundation piers can be easily pieced; and as a result, instead of a low, dark cellar, a light, airy basement is obtained. If now the floor is concreted with cement this basement can serve for a laundry, for storage-room, and also for whatever heating apparatus is adopted. The walls and the ceiling of the cellar should be well whitewashed.

After the cellar probably the attic will need most attention. That also is apt to be low and dark and unserviceable. But by cutting through the roof for large dormer-windows, by laying a new floor on the old rough boards, and then by painting or lime-washing the walls and roof, a fine dormitory can be had, which increases greatly the capacity of the house.

Not much needs to be done to the rooms on the first and second floors. If any old fireplaces have been bricked up it is easy to knock down the false-work. If any paper still hangs on the walls, that is to be scraped off, and the ceilings and walls are to be painted so that they can be easily washed. Soft wood floors must also be painted, after careful filling of all cracks with putty, or even first calking with oakum.

The comfort of patients will be greatly heightened if broad piazzas are available. And, besides steps leading down to the grass, there should also be an incline for rolling-chairs. Nothing is so helpful in restoring the spirits of a convalescent as to roll him out of doors on a wheeled chair, or even on his bed. And then, if he can be so taken out on the grass, under the trees, that tonic is of wonderful effect.

The most important, and probably the most expensive, improvements that must be made in the old house come under the head of heating and plumbing. For the heating a first-rate furnace will answer. Care must be taken that the cold-air supply for it comes through a perfectly tight shaft, so that no cellar-air shall enter the wards, as we must now call the refitted rooms. And the furnace ought to be of the kind that allows separate currents, not merely from the common heating-chamber of the furnace, but all the way from the cold-air supply. Only in this way can the even heating of the house be secured in different winds. And the furnace should be of such capacity that it will never be necessary to close the ventilators in order to keep the house warm.

Where there are open fireplaces these will serve as ventilators. If a little fire in each would be too much, then a common lamp burning in it will create an upward ventilating current. Where there are no fireplaces or no unused chimney-flues which can be cut into, special ventilating-pipes must be put in. This is as necessary as the introduction of hot-air pipes from the furnace; for hot air or fresh cold air cannot be made to enter a room unless some way is provided for the escape of the air already in. Great ingenuity may be required to provide this ventilating system. If the ventilating-pipes can be grouped and led into one large shaft, then by heating the air in this shaft with a gas or kerosene stove sure ventilating currents can be secured. In close weather, when there is no furnace fire, this especially heated ventilating apparatus becomes a necessity. For in no other way can fresh air be induced into the fever-laden wards.

If any rooms must necessarily be heated separately, Franklin stoves are good substitutes for fireplaces. Where there is not even a chimney flue available, the " St. Louis Ventilating Fresh-air Heater "* is a most satisfactory apparatus.

A plentiful supply of good water is an absolute necessity in a hospital. If, unfortunately, there is at hand no public supply, then wells and windmill-pumps, or at any rate a large tank in the attic, and powerful hand force-pumps, must be provided. Unless the necessary plumbing can easily be introduced into the house it may be cheaper as well as better to build an adjoining tower for all the water-works. This would almost surely be less expensive than to tear the house to pieces, as plumbers seem to delight in doing, where bathrooms and water-closets and wash-sinks have to be provided only for one floor. And even where there are two floors, the men's wards below and the women's above, to be provided, still, if there is any easy way of connecting this water-works tower with

---

* Made and sold by E. F. Crosby, Brookline, Mass.

the house, it may be the least expensive way, and always it is the best way. If this tower plan is adopted the laundry can be incorporated in it, thus relieving the cellar, and avoiding the expense and trouble of properly ventilating a basement laundry.

The patients' bathtubs ought to be on wheels, that the tubs may be carried full to the bedsides, and then wheeled back to their places for emptying.

Where no suitable house can be found for transformation into a hospital, and, instead, a small ordinary dwelling with plenty of unoccupied land is secured, then the task of providing a temporary hospital is plainer and pleasanter.

To begin with the house itself, that needs almost no alteration. If in fairly good repair, it will do at once for the general kitchen, for the office and living-rooms of the matron and head nurse, for the store-rooms of hospital supplies; in short, for the administration building. And, besides, there will perhaps be rooms in it for private patients or for convalescents.

Two wards, one for male the other for female patients, can be built, one on each side of the administration or "centre" building, and connected therewith by corridors.

Each ward, being of one story and not intended for a permanent building, can be lightly framed. There is no need of a cellar. And to prevent the floor from cold, a lathed and rough-plastered ceiling should be laid below the floor-beams. This must, of course, be carried out flush with the outer walls. The inside finish should be of ordinary plastering carried up to the ridge.

These wards may be of any desired size, but, whether

for few or many patients, each should be so divided as to have separate rooms in one half and an open ward in the other. The nurse in charge must have a room there for her medicines and supplies. And often patients are too sick or too troublesome for the open ward. Then, too, when the end is nigh a separate room is of utmost importance.

A chimney and open fireplace for a ward is a great luxury. An open stove with its smoke-pipe carried up through the roof is equally good and far less expensive. But for the uniform heating of such a ward there is no better way than the hot-water system, used in greenhouses and fast coming into use in our best buildings. By using this system both wards, and the centre house as well, can be heated from one fire. The apparatus can be put in the house cellar, and the pipes, properly protected, carried thence out to the wards, around their walls, just under the windows, and then back under the floors to the central apparatus.

The chief objection to this system of heating is that it does not provide any fresh supply of air. It is therefore necessary to arrange for a separate system of ventilation. Apertures can be made in the walls, just opposite the heating-pipes, with registers in them for allowing the entrance of fresh air, which will become more or less warmed by passing the hot-water pipes.

The familiar window ventilating-screens can also be employed. And for the egress of air from the wards special ventilators should be made in the gables and also in the roof.

To complete this temporary hospital it is now only necessary to arrange for the water-works. All the sinks, laundry-tubs, bathrooms, and water-closets may best be put in a separate building, easily accessible by short corridors both from each ward and from the centre building.

Either of these plans for a temporary hospital would lead to a happy result; neither requires a great expenditure of money nor a long delay; and, by adopting either, the hospital work may soon be well begun. But if for any reason neither of these plans can be adopted, even so let there be no faint-heartedness in providing the best accommodations that can be afforded. Once having taken hold of the plough-handles, go on.

In order to make the temporary hospital ready for all kinds of work, some extra provision must be made for the treatment of cases of contagious diseases. For such cases an isolated ward is necessary. It need not be far off, but it must be entirely separate from the other buildings, and it must itself be a miniature hospital; for in it the nurses must stay, as well as the patients, and all the housekeeping work has to be done there.

A small cottage will serve the purpose fairly well. It will only occasionally have to be used for cases of contagious disease, for such diseases, happily, are not always attacking the community. And when not so used, it will be better for the cottage to let some of the nurses or servants, or even the convalescent patients, live there. Then at an hour's notice, if needed for a scarlet-fever patient, it could be made ready, and this more surely than if it stood entirely vacant for most of the time.

There is no doubt that it is now possible to disinfect

thoroughly a room or a house after its occupancy by patients suffering from any of the contagious diseases. It is possible also to disinfect clothing and furniture; but not always without damage to the disinfected articles. For this disinfection dry heat or steam heat is the best agent. And no contagious-disease hospital would be complete without some apparatus for disinfecting contaminated material. A brick chamber, say in the cellar of the cottage, might be made, with a small steam-boiler near by, so arranged as to keep the chamber either full of live steam, or at an equally high dry heat, for hours if need be. Such a "sterilizing oven" would be of great use to the other parts of the hospital, in renovating mattresses and in disinfecting other articles of furniture.

The proper furnishing of a hospital is not a difficult task. There are no carpets, no hangings, no fancy articles of any kind, to be bought. Everything must be plain and substantial.

The bedsteads are the only articles of peculiar design. These should be of very strong iron construction, and higher than the ordinary cot.

The mattress should be of best curled hair. Nothing can be too good in the way of bed for those who have to stay on it both day and night. Each bed has to have a rubber protecting sheet.

The blankets and sheets, the pillows and counterpanes, must all be of best quality; for nothing of poor quality will stand the wear of the necessary washing.

Plain bureaus and wardrobes and open wash-stands, a few plain chairs, and some small, simple tables complete the list of needed furniture. Everything must be of such design that it can be kept clean, wiped over in every part with a dampened cloth, at the least possible expenditure of time and strength.

The table and kitchen furnishings, as well as the furniture for the office and officers' living-rooms, can of course be of any style. But the china to be used on the patients' trays ought to correspond with fickle appetites. A nurse cannot serve tempting tidbits in heavy, thick ware.

The accumulation of strictly hospital material need not bother the managers. That can be safely left to the matron, who, if she knows her business, will know where and in what forms to buy it most advantageously. But in order to be businesslike from the start, no bills for furnishings or for hospital material ought to be paid out of the hospital treasury which have not been approved by the managers as well as by the matron.

In furnishing a hospital it is customary to make special appeals to individuals or to societies for the furniture of special rooms, or for some special articles. In this way beautiful memorials have been founded. All such gifts should, however, be made only upon consultation with the housekeeping committee, in order to insure the necessary uniformity.

One of the costly and yet very desirable possessions for a hospital is an ambulance. Even where there is no hospital, such a vehicle, constructed for the easiest carriage of the sick and injured, is occasionally a great comfort and blessing. Where there is a hospital, an ambulance becomes almost a necessity. And the need of it offers to those who might give it a fine opportunity for generous giving.

The ambulance should be kept at some central stable, where its services can be quickly had when needed.

CHAPTER VII.

THE ADMISSION OF PATIENTS.—NECESSARY REGULATIONS.

WHILE the temporary hospital is being made ready the managers will have ample opportunity for determining the general policy of the hospital, and for drafting the rules and regulations by which its work shall be governed.

Those who have expected that it will be possible for the hospital to fulfil every need will have to suffer some disappointment. Thus in a general hospital it is not advisable to take in patients suffering with chronic diseases. The beds ought rather to be reserved for patients who at least have a chance of being cured, or for patients who otherwise would die or suffer longer and more keenly; and yet it is very hard to rule out the helpless old man whose last sickness is upon him.

In large cities there are homes for the aged and helpless, and special hospitals for consumptives and for those afflicted with cancer, and asylums for those, most unfortunate of all, who have lost their minds. But in a small city, while there is equal variety of suffering, there are not enough patients in the different classes to make separate provision for them possible. A small hospital should therefore be more general in the character of its work than a large hospital can be, without interfering with its main mission. But even so, for the sake of all concerned, it will not do to fill the beds with consumptives, and then not have room for the victims of accident, for the sufferers from acute diseases, and for those whose lives depend upon having hospital care after some needed surgical operation. And then, besides, if the hospital is nearly full of patients who can never leave it alive, there is in that very fact an inevitable depression; and soon there will be a general fear of being carried there.

Some forms of disease are also so annoying or so offensive to those in the immediate neighborhood of the patient that even well people can hardly endure the strain. Patients so afflicted might be helped in the hospital, but other patients there would suffer.

Again, on the other hand, in many cases of chronic disease it is often possible by proper treatment to bring the patients into much more comfortable condition, and indeed to prolong their lives. This is especially true in cases of consumption. And this disease in most localities is more prevalent, as well as more fatal, than all other infectious diseases put together. It would be an inestimable service to the community if every consumptive could be given a season of hospital treatment, and there taught how to take care of himself properly, and at least how to prevent the infection of others. Were this done, not a few would be cured; many would be greatly relieved, and their lives and usefulness prolonged: all would be made more comfortable.

If consumptives, or patients suffering from other chronic disease, are admitted for only a definite period;

and if care is taken to discharge them, when they have improved as much as they probably will there, or when it is evident that they are failing,—then the hospital can do much good, and yet not suffer, as inevitably it would suffer, were chronic cases admitted to stay as long as they might live.

It is thus manifest that the usefulness of the hospital greatly depends upon the class of patients admitted. And in framing the regulations this question becomes the first for consideration.

Large hospitals have a resident medical officer who can decide upon the admission of patients. But even there some regulations must express the policy of the hospital in this matter. In the small hospital there is no resident medical officer. Nor is it fair to leave much responsibility of this kind to the matron. In emergencies she may admit a patient; but it is as outside her rightful province to diagnosticate diseases as to decide questions of the general policy of the hospital.

One of the medical staff, or one of the physicians belonging to the board of managers, may well serve as the admitting officer. In this way the matron can be relieved of much responsibility. Only when the urgency is great, and where there can be no doubt of the propriety of admitting a patient, need she admit except with a permission in writing from the admitting officer.

So far we have considered this question of the admissibility of patients only in its medical aspects. That is of most importance. But the question is also to be considered from the financial point of view.

The charity of the hospital must always be strictly reserved for those in absolute need of it. Even if only so used, it will be hard enough to collect the money needed. Patients who can pay the cost of their support should certainly be required so to do; and those who can pay only a part should also be required to pay what they can. There is great opportunity here for mistaken kindness on the part of the authorities. For to very few in this world is sickness not a direct money hardship; and it seems heartless to take from the sick man his few saved-up dollars. But it is not the hospital's mission to ease the financial burdens of people. Let other charities do that. The hospital's mission is to relieve and comfort the sick and suffering, to help all curative processes, and to do this alike for the rich and poor. And in order to be able to do this for the poor money must be solicited. This is trust money: it is given for an especial purpose, and that purpose must ever be held in view.

Nor is it sufficient observance of the obligations of the trust to admit to the hospital as a free patient one whose family or employer is morally bound, and also perfectly able, to pay the cost of his care. In deciding in such cases the managers must not follow their own personally generous impulses: they must remember that the hospital funds have been entrusted to them for the support of the friendless poor, of the absolutely impoverished.

And when it is remembered that the patients who pay to the hospital full cost pay really much less than they would have to pay for lodging and board and nursing of any kind outside; and further, that much more is given them than twice as much money would buy for them anywhere, except in a hospital,—then it does not seem such a hardship to require of all who can pay that they should do so. But it is a most distasteful business, this hunting into patients' ability to pay, and it is the part of the managers' business most often neglected. Nevertheless it is a grand opportunity for real useful service. As its importance is recognized perhaps some one of the managers will volunteer to help the hospital by bringing to the treasurer or to the executive committee all possible information concerning the financial ability of applicants for free beds in the hospital, or for rebates from the cost charges. Such rebates and admissions to free beds should be granted only by the executive committee, and only upon fullest information.

Now comes the task of summing up in one rule these restrictions, and others that may be locally advisable, regarding the admission of patients. The following attempt may serve as an example:

REGULATION I.—ADMISSION OF PATIENTS.

1. Patients applying for admission to the Utopia Hospital must present to the matron a recommendation from the admitting physician, Dr. So-and-so [residence and office hours here to be given], and also satisfactory evidence of their ability and willingness to pay the hospital charges of ten dollars per week.

2. Patients desiring admission to free beds, or rebates of the regular charges, after obtaining the recommendation of the admitting physician, must apply for the same to Mrs. Blank [residence here to be given]. In making this application applicants must give all particulars of their needs, for the information of the executive committee. Every patient is expected to pay as much as can possibly be afforded towards the cost of his care.

3. Patients suffering from mental diseases or from alcoholism will not be admitted. Patients suffering from chronic diseases will be admitted only for temporary treatment. In cases of accident or other emergency, patients may be admitted at the discretion of the matron.

In the chapters upon the medical question and upon nursing-service the different policies possible, and also the best to adopt, were fully discussed. In order to bring these policies plainly into view, we will now try to incorporate them in regulation shape.

REGULATION II.—SURGICAL AND MEDICAL ATTENDANCE.

1. Patients desiring the service of any particular surgeon or physician are at liberty to engage the same, just as they would in their own homes. But in case the patient is the recipient of hospital charity, it must be understood that no professional charge is to be made or paid.

2. Patients having no choice as to their professional attendance will be attended gratuitously by the members of the hospital staff, serving in rotation.

3. Patients desiring homœopathic treatment, upon so informing the matron, will be furnished with the same.

4. Changes in professional attendance will not be allowed, except with the sanction of the medical committee of the managers. Requests therefor may be made through the matron.

REGULATION III.—THE NURSING-SERVICE.

1. The nursing-service is entrusted to the Utopia Training-school for Nurses.

2. All nurses, as well as all other employés of the hospital, are under the direction of the matron. The implicit, immediate, and cheerful obedience of all is especially enjoined. Any failure therein will lead to the dismissal of the offender from the hospital's service.

These three regulations ought to cover fairly well the general policy of the hospital. As for the rules by which the actual work is done, these should be left for the matron to evolve. The rules, as well as the regulations, should be printed, and always given to those concerned.

CHAPTER VIII.

THE PERMANENT HOSPITAL BUILDINGS.—HOW TO PLAN AND HOW TO BUILD THEM.

AFTER spending considerable money and much time and attention upon a temporary hospital, it is perhaps asking too much of the ordinary mortal to think seriously of the subject of a permanent hospital. And yet no harm can result, and possibly great good may come, by beginning early to study plans and methods of building. In growing towns it is important, too, to secure the best possible location, before land becomes too expensive for allowing to the hospital a generous area of surrounding lawn.

Then it must be remembered that the temporary hospital is only a makeshift, and that better work can be done in buildings designed and built for the purpose. Nor need it be so very long before the permanent hospital may be begun. Some rich men may be even now ready to give largely to it, or some wills may be drawn in the hospital's favor, and large bequests may come unheralded. This latter event is more likely to happen if the hospital people push on their good work to completion. And in order to do this intelligently it is necessary to know what others have done elsewhere.

The reports published by hospitals lately built generally give sketch plans of their buildings, and also some description. The only satisfactory way of studying the subject of hospital building is to visit all the new hospitals within easy reach.

Every one interested in the hospital movement should make it a point, whenever in another city or hospital town, to visit and to study the methods employed there, and also the construction of the buildings. Notes should be freely taken, and kept within easy reach. In this way a large collective fund of information can be gathered, which will help greatly towards making the new hospital the best in the world —as indeed the newest hospital ought always to be.

Twenty years or so ago the idea was prevalent that hospital wards should always be of such cheap construction that they could be replaced every few years with fresh buildings of like temporary structure. This idea in the light of present knowledge is a frightful one. For, supposing a ward must necessarily become contaminated, this is as likely to happen in the first month as it is after several years of use. Or, in other words, such a ward after its first use might always be a source of danger. And then, besides the unavoidable extravagance of this way of doing, there would of necessity be a sacrifice of every structural convenience that could be dispensed with. Indeed, as has been mentioned, the sanitariness of the wards would be jeopardized by the cheapness of the construction. And this is enough said; for the whole intent of hospital construction is to secure the highest possible sanitary quality, together with such conveniences of arrangement as will allow the greatest economy in administration.

In one sense this is the architect's business. But

architects do not usually know much about hospitals, for they do not have to build many; and it is unlikely that an architect can be found for the Utopia Hospital who has ever before built one. And however this may be, the hospital organization before engaging an architect ought to have very definite ideas of what sort of buildings are wanted.

All preliminary consideration of the problem, as well as the immediate supervision of the plans, and finally of the building process, can best be done by a committee appointed for the purpose by the corporation.

The problem of determining the general plan best adapted to the particular conditions in any given case is in reality the very problem that most demands expert study and advice, and can be considered intelligently only by those who have made themselves familiar with the various requirements of a model hospital. Let us then consider these different requirements.

It is fitting to think first of the operating-room and its accessories. Grewsome as the subject seems to those who would never know of the world's woes, yet to those who know how much suffering is relieved and how many lives are saved by modern surgery the subject of providing suitable facilities for it is intensely interesting. No other part of the hospital is of so great importance. Severely simple and plain these rooms must be; but the lighting, heating, ventilating, and plumbing arrangements must be perfect.

Besides the operating-room itself, even in a small hospital, there should be an adjoining dressing-room and wash-room for the surgeons; a room for drugs and supplies; an etherizing-room; and an accident ward for the reception and preliminary treatment of such patients. Thus five or six rooms are needed for what may be called the surgical suite.

This set of rooms, while in one sense making the important centre of the hospital, should be well away from the wards, and also so separate from the main building as not to allow, on one hand, the transmission of the ether fumes or of the patient's outcries, or, on the other hand, the entrance into the operating-room of the dust and noise of the administration-rooms and hallways. A very good way of obtaining this desirable isolation would be to group these rooms in a one-story wing leading out of the central building.

The operating-room itself must be thus built, for that room must have skylights, as well as one of its sides practically of glass. Adjoining the operating-room a large wash-room is needed, and then, beyond that, a dressing-room for the surgeons.

The room for drugs and for surgical supplies, if large enough to allow glass cases on the sides for the storage of these articles, can also well serve as the preparation-room, where all surgical material can be sterilized. For this work bench-tables and sinks may be placed in the centre of the room. This room, and also the accident ward, must be well lighted. The etherizing and the consulting rooms need no special provisions; nor, indeed, need they be immediately adjoining the others of this suite.

Passing now to the wards, it will be easier to make plain what arrangements are desirable. Each ward should lead off from the administration building by a corridor, which, as it nears the ward, should be especially its own. If there are to be many wards, one may be made up of small single rooms opening out of a centre hallway; and other wards may be open throughout their extent, except for the nurses' office, one or two separate isolating-rooms, and the supply-room, at one end. But if there are to be only two or three ward wings, then it will be most convenient to have in each more of the space allotted to separate rooms, for these purposes. For patients often need separate accommodation, as when too sick to bear the necessary noise or temperature or light of the general ward, and when for many reasons their presence in the ward would disturb and distress other occupants.

The best place for the housekeeping work of a small hospital, for the kitchen, and perhaps also for the laundry, is in the top story of the administration building. There is thus secured the greatest freedom from the odors and steam, and also the greatest convenience in distributing the food to the wards by means of a light-weighted lift from the tea-kitchens below.

It is not within the province of this chapter to discuss the details of the arrangement or of the construction of the different parts of the hospital. But it may serve the general purpose to point out some of the requirements in these respects that naturally provoke most astonishment upon first consideration. Thus in the matter of permanence, which has already received some attention, it must be remembered that the hospital building and all its fixtures will receive vastly more wear from legitimate usage than will any private dwelling. The work of the hospital is to be continuous, both by night and by day, for years and for generations after its builders shall be gathered to their fathers. No material can therefore be too durable for employment in its construction. Especially does this fact apply to those parts which if their integrity is impaired would jeopardize the sanitary quality of the hospital. Thus the plumbing must necessarily be the best obtainable regardless of cost. And, again, because of this certainty of long use, and with respect to true economy, there must be full as many sinks and bowls and other plumbing conveniences as can be used. Saving in this would be a lasting wastefulness of labor. And what would be lavish provision in a private residence would be entirely insufficient provision for a hospital. In no other department, with possible exception of the heating and ventilating systems, is there such imperative need of expert advice as to plans and supervision of the workmanship.

Returning now to the general plan for the arrangement of the different parts of the hospital, it may be laid down as an axiom that the best arrangement is that of a central or administration building, with semi-detached wings for wards and for the surgical suite. This general plan, or pavilion-plan as it is called, allows great diversity of arrangement in order best to adapt the buildings to local conditions.

The building committee must become accustomed to looking far into the future. They must always keep in mind that what they will build is only a nucleus of a far larger institution, and therefore must be so arranged as to allow for this extension with greatest advantage. Fortunately this requirement also is admirably met by the pavilion-plan.

So far as the outside of the buildings is concerned, while there is no danger in having that ornamented according to taste, yet it is not to be forgotten that there is beauty in severe simplicity, and that the greatest success in architecture, even from the æsthetic standpoint, depends upon the perfect adaptability of the buildings to their especial purposes.

In deciding upon the size of a permanent hospital the probable growth of the town is the factor needing most consideration. That, of course, is not accurately determinable. But it can be well guessed at. And the hospital ought to be planned for at least fifty years' service without change of its general plan. This can be effected by making the central building large enough to serve all the wards which it is expected will be needed for fifty years to come; and by so arranging the wards that others can be added without interfering with those first built. The size of the temporary hospital, and the numbers of patients during successive years, will give the best information as to the size needed for the permanent hospital, which, because of its greater advantages, will of course have to be even at the beginning larger than the temporary hospital. In some communities hospitals need to be relatively larger than in others. No general rule of much value can be given. Probably one hospital bed for every five hundred is a better rule than one bed for every thousand inhabitants.

The size as well as the construction of the hospital depends in the first instance upon the amount of money available for building. It will never do, however, to let this consideration govern the planning. The business of the building committee is to procure the best possible plans for what is needed. The soliciting committees can then work for some definite object. If there appears no possibility of securing enough to build by these plans, then it is soon enough to modify them.

The search for money to build with is a task separate from all other soliciting. If a community contributes enough money to fit up a temporary hospital and to carry that along, it is useless to ask for enough more to build a permanent building. The city government might do it by taxing the people, but that is a poor way for the city and for the hospital as well. It seems to be almost the only way in this country of securing such a boon to enlist the interest of the wealthy and to obtain the needed funds from a comparatively few donors. The beautiful idea of making these small hospitals or parts of them memorials for those "loved long since and lost awhile" is sure to gain more and more in favor. Living memorials in continuous use are so incomparably above all useless piles of stone.

CHAPTER IX.

THE HOSPITAL FINANCES.—HOSPITAL AID ASSOCIATIONS.—HOSPITAL SUNDAY AND HOSPITAL SATURDAY COLLECTIONS. — ENDOWMENTS. — FREE BEDS.—PUBLIC APPROPRIATIONS.

FOR enthusiasts who are acquainted with the good work of hospitals in relieving the sufferings of humanity it is often a dreary, perplexing question why it is so hard to raise the money necessary for the work. There can be no doubt the money would always be forthcoming were the need of it and the right use of it widely known. This, then, is the first task before the finance committee—to show forth both the need of money and the economical use of it in the hospital. For this purpose the businesslike balance-sheets of the treasurer are useful only to the very few who can read them. Most people need more simple statements. They can understand the cost per week of groceries, of milk, and of ice; they know, too, how essential these expenses are. And some will contribute towards one of the special expenses of the hospital when they could not be induced to help swell the general expense fund. Indeed, the treasurer's statement that he has left for running expenses only a few hundred dollars carries no sort of appeal to those who never have many dollars ahead. But those same people will often willingly give a dollar or two to supply some thoroughly understood want.

The expenses of the hospital should therefore be analyzed by the finance committee, and presented to the public through the local papers or by leaflet statements in the most simple and intelligible way. If the children realize that a few pennies from each in the school will allow some sick child to be fed and tenderly nursed in the hospital for a few days or weeks, the little scholars will save their pennies, and then, in giving them in charity's sweet name, they will have learned a real lesson.

And in the same way their parents, who perhaps have never formed the habit of giving, may be led to share their children's joy if it is presented to them what blessings their few dollars will afford to the helpless sick.

In like manner the work done by the hospital ought to be made generally known, not only in the tables of the annual report, which few read and still fewer understand, but also in more readable form. The particular story of the care given to some sick stranger will interest people who would care nothing about the composite story of twenty such cases. And these particular stories can be given out frequently. This is an advantage; for the public cares little about things seldom heard of.

It is not enough to give such information only by the printer's types. Valuable as the printed reports may be, such means should be supplemented by direct speech. All interested in the hospital's success should take every opportunity to enlist the interest of others. And those who can tell the story in an interesting way to companies of people should always be ready to tell it. Such personal appeals are often the most effective of all.

In giving all possible information to the public, both as to the need of continuous gifts of money and also as to the work that is done with the money as given, the managers of the hospital really are doing all that can fairly be expected of them. They are immediately concerned in the right expenditure of these trust funds. And it is only right that they should receive help in the raising of the money.

Another distinct organization for this especial purpose is very desirable. In many hospital towns there is this Hospital Aid Association, and it is an admirable institution. Such an association may naturally grow out of the company that first holds a fair or festival for the hospital's benefit; or from some circle of generous women who meet to do the sewing needed. It soon is plain that it is easier to hold over than it is to form new organizations each season as needed.

As the work done for the hospital by such an association increases, it becomes advisable to effect a suitable organization. At first it is better that the meetings should be entirely informal. Ladies then like to attend the meetings; and interest in the association's work grows apace. Many of the hospital managers will take part, and often some of the surgeons or the matron can attend the meetings and tell what is going on. Often, too, the association can be invited to the hospital to see what the work there really is. In such ways a deep, abiding interest in hospital work can be created and fostered.

One great boon of having such an auxiliary association is that it can decide what sort of means shall be employed each year for providing the hospital's support. Fairs and festivals, benefit concerts and balls, are all very well in due season; but if such affairs come too often people soon tire of the sound of the word charity. And yet when some club offers an entertainment to be given under the auspices of the hospital, it is a very ungracious thing to have to decline the offer. The predicament is escaped most neatly by referring the offer to the Hospital Aid Association, which can arrange such matters with due regard to the pleasure of the public.

There are several well-recognized ways of raising the money for hospital support, which we will now consider one by one. First, the Hospital Sunday collections. The church as a whole is the largest body to which appeal can be made for any good work. And it certainly seems very fitting that one Sunday of the year should be devoted by the church to a recognition of the Christian work of hospitals, and to exertions in its behalf. This fitness is generally recognized, and the churches are very willing to coöperate. But considerable arranging is necessary to bring about the institution of the custom. The churches must each be asked long in advance, as in many churches arrangements as to the disposition of the Sunday collections are made for a year ahead. Different churches prefer different seasons for such a collection. And it is no small task to bring about a general agreement. After that is effected, and a certain Sunday is designated, every effort should be made to make this a permanent custom, otherwise the work of arranging has to be repeated each year. Nor is it sufficient to obtain the consent of every church to the arrangement; for what is not made some one's particular business is apt to be neglected. Clergymen and church officials are constantly changing, and what one promises another forgets to do. And if the custom is to prevail some committee must attend to these details. This committee can best be appointed by the Hospital Aid Association. Their business will be to make sure that every clergyman is interested in the hospital and understands its work. If one has not seen it, let some of the committee take him there and explain its work. Then this information, and the statements of expenses and of needs for the coming year, should be given on printed or written slips to each clergyman several weeks before Hospital Sunday. During the week before that day public appeals should be made, with the request that those who cannot conveniently contribute in the churches should send their subscriptions directly to the hospital authorities, or through the hands of their pastors or church treasurers. As soon afterwards as possible the treasurer of the hospital ought to make a public announcement of the contributions received from each source. And this statement ought to be republished a few weeks before the next Hospital Sunday.

In order effectively to reach the non-churchgoers, several plans may be suggested. One plan, which works very successfully in the large cities of England, is that of Hospital Saturday collections. The Saturday chosen for this work should be several months distant from the Hospital Sunday, in order not to interfere with the full success of either day's collections. The same preliminary work must be done of calling general attention to the needs of the hospital, and to the particular day appointed for the collections. A special committee for managing the matter is also needed. Well-known persons—and the more prominent they are the better for the success of the scheme—have to be secured to take charge of the collection-boxes, which may be stationed in the most accessible places for different wards or districts. Thus stations should be established at factory doors, in the post-office, at the railway-stations, or wherever many persons will pass during the few hours appointed for the collecting. And as soon as the treasurer receives the collections the returns should be made public.

Still another plan for reaching all is that of the soliciting canvass. By this plan a large number of volunteer solicitors, among whom the town is divided up into sections,—one section for each solicitor,—undertake to ask a subscription from every individual in the community. In order to make this canvass effective, the solicitors ought to be assembled for full instructions. Every solicitor must have at tongue's end the reasons for asking for money, and in fact a general knowledge of what the hospital is doing. For many inquiries will be made of them, and all sorts of criticisms of the hospital will be poured into the solicitors' ears instead of money into their boxes. If, however, the solicitors are well informed, in this way a general knowledge of the hospital is publicly diffused, in itself a most desirable result.

Success by this method depends upon the number of volunteer canvassers and upon their hearty work. At the start, and when the public interest is especially aroused, many will volunteer for this work and do it well. But in the natural course of things it will probably always become necessary to supplement this volunteer work by that of paid canvassers. Many who would like to work in this way really cannot afford to give the requisite time, but if paid fairly for it they can help both themselves and the hospital. Such canvassers are under better control than unpaid ones. They can be given the districts to work in where volunteers fail.

By combining with this plan of a general canvass the advantages of the "envelope" or pledge system, probably the most satisfactory results will be obtained.

Each solicitor will ask not only for one subscription, but will also ask for a pledge of another like subscription at some appointed future date. On obtaining this promise the solicitor will leave with the one thus promising an envelope with the amount pledged, and also the date on which the pledge is due plainly printed on it. The solicitor then returns to the committee in charge the money collected, and also the names and addresses of those who have taken envelopes of the different denominations. And when the next appointed day arrives, the same solicitor or another calls on those who have taken envelopes for the amounts pledged.

Instead of envelopes thus distributed in accordance with the pledges, the names of all willing to contribute yearly or quarterly or monthly may be recorded in books specially designed for the purpose. With these books the canvassers can make the stated collections.

Where this plan of collecting is adopted besides the large amount gained there is the advantage of having a basis for estimating what the yearly income of the hospital will be. In every mercantile enterprise, and in every household, reasonable prudence requires the limiting of expenses within the estimated income. In hospital management such prudence would smooth the pathway of the finance committee, but unfortunately it is seldom possible. And any system of collecting subscriptions, by which closer estimates of the probable income can be made, will highly commend itself to the managers.

We have now considered two sources of a hospital's income—the revenue from patients able to pay, wholly or in part, the cost of their stay, and the annual contributions of the public. Each of these sources yields a varying income. And it is almost necessary that the hospital shall have some portion of its income a certainty. To this end it is very desirable that an endowment fund be established either in the form of a general fund or in the form of special endowments for the support of free beds. The latter form appeals more strongly to those who wish to create memorials; and also to those who are liable to want to send their employés as patients to the hospital.

But, after all, the matter of free beds in a hospital is more or less of a fiction. For no particular beds are thus designated, and the hospital rules regulate the admissions in all cases. It is, however, a common practice in hospitals to accept as free patients all who are sent by those who have given free-bed endowments or annual subscriptions affording equal income. And where a free bed is established for the benefit of a certain class, as for instance the operatives in some particular factory, the managers are enabled to be especially liberal in the acceptance of such as free patients.

Special privileges may with propriety be given to donors of free beds; for it is the hospital's business to furnish what is especially wanted by those who support it.

The only other source of certain revenue is that of a possible annual grant from the city government, or, better still, a contract with the city whereby a certain allowance shall be paid to the hospital for every patient cared for who otherwise would surely be a public charge. Such an arrangement is of great advantage both to the city and to the hospital. The city is thereby relieved of carrying on an almshouse hospital, which is an unfailing source of extravagance to the city and of misery to the sick poor; and at the same time the hospital is assured of a part of the expense of caring for those who can pay nothing.

Whatever money arrangements are made with the city, the hospital should never allow any dictation as to its own management. As a proper compliment to the powers that be, it is all very well to have the mayor of the city or some one of the town's officers a member *ex officio* of the hospital corporation. But only those who have an earnest, deep interest in hospital work should ever be intrusted with its management.

Part II.

SUGGESTIONS

FOR

HOSPITAL ARCHITECTURE,

WITH

PLANS FOR A SMALL HOSPITAL.

BY

WILLIAM ATKINSON, Architect.

HOSPITAL ARCHITECTURE.

It is the province of hospital architecture to provide for the collective treatment of sick and wounded persons, and to promote, as far as planning and construction of buildings can do so, their comfort and restoration to health. The excellence of a hospital does not consist in the proportions of its façade, or the profiles of its mouldings; it is to be sought for in the records of mortality and cure within its walls. From the preliminary studies to the last details of construction, the sanitary aspect of the problem should be uppermost in the mind of the designer.

The following suggestions, while applicable to hospitals of any description, are more especially intended for those built on the "pavilion plan," of detached buildings of a single story, either entirely separated from one another, or connected by means of open or partially enclosed corridors.

From the architect's point of view the planning of a hospital resolves itself into three parts: (1) the general arrangement of the buildings on the site; (2) the planning of the individual members of the group; and (3) the design of details, including methods and materials of construction, and the heating, ventilating, and plumbing systems.

In the arrangement of the buildings on the site we should endeavor—

(1) To secure a large amount of sunlight for each one;

(2) To impede as little as possible the circulation of air in and around the buildings;

(3) To provide for the future enlargement of the hospital; and

(4) To promote convenience and economy of administration.

To study properly the question of sunlight, a "sun plan" of the buildings must be drawn, and their positions considered with reference to the shadows they cast upon each other and upon the ground. An astronomical table, showing the path of the sun, from sunrise to sunset at the different seasons of the year, is desirable for this work. The length of a shadow cast by an object being in proportion to the height of the object, it follows that low buildings, with flat roofs, are to be preferred to high buildings and roofs of steep pitch, entirely apart from other considerations. Flat roofs also allow of overhead lighting of the rooms below. Skylights or monitors may be placed anywhere upon their surface, and the sunlight thus let into rooms which otherwise might get none.*

The buildings should be placed so as to offer as little obstruction as possible to a free movement of air in and around them. Projections from the general surface of a wall, forming sheltered angles, in which air may stagnate; quadrangles enclosed on all sides, or

---

* The term "flat roof" is used here in its usual sense, and means a roof of exceedingly gentle pitch, generally about half an inch to the foot.

blind courts, with no outlet for the pocketed air, are bad features in any hospital design.

The buildings occupied by the sick should be located away from all possible sources of noise, and the windows of the wards should command an agreeable prospect, and not be subject to the observation of curious neighbors. .

The general ground plan of the hospital will of necessity be largely governed by local conditions—such as the nature of the surface, the character of neighboring buildings, the possibilities of acquiring adjoining properties for future growth, and the like. Such conditions often necessitate a departure from an ideal arrangement.

In designing the individual buildings the aim should be to satisfy the requirements with the simplest floor-plan obtainable, and to avoid a multiplicity of angles. Every unnecessary corner adds so much extra labor to the task of keeping the building clean.

There should be abundant light in every part. Passages and hallways should be straight, and capable of being opened at both ends, to allow of quick ventilation.

For the ward pavilions, buildings of a single story are preferable, and each pavilion should contain but one principal sick-ward, with its adjuncts. In this way only can a complete isolation of the different classes of patients be obtained.

Where limitations of site make the use of two-story pavilions desirable, the upper and lower wards should be, as far as possible, isolated from each other. No channel of communication, by dumb-waiter shafts, ventilating-flues, or the like should be allowed between them. The stairways to the upper ward should be built outside the walls of the building or in a staircase well opening to the outer air. The floors between should be made absolutely sound-proof, and ample means of escape, in case of fire, must be provided for the upper ward.

The ward windows should have square tops and extend clear up to the ceiling. The arched form of window is unsuitable for hospital construction, as it curtails the light at the point where it is most valuable. The sills should be low enough for the patients to see out of the windows from their beds, and the floor-level should be sufficiently above the outside grade to prevent people outside from looking in. The blinds or window-screens should be arranged in two parts, to pull up from the bottom and down from the top. By this arrangement the distribution of light within the ward may be more exactly controlled.

In the design of details one of the chief considerations is the avoidance of lodging-places for dust and dirt. Air is constantly passing through a building, more or less according to the efficiency of the ventilation, and in its passage leaves behind a certain percentage of its dust. A building acts as a sort of gigantic air-filter, and tends to accumulate dust, year by year, exactly as a water-filter becomes clogged with particles. Dust is also brought in from outside on the clothing of the inmates, and is also produced to a certain extent within the building itself.

The greater part of this dust settles on horizontal surfaces, but vertical surfaces also collect a certain amount. Even such a smooth material as window-glass becomes clouded in time with impalpable dust particles.

The aim of the designer should be to reduce the amount of dust-collecting surface, and to render such surface accessible, so that the dust may be periodically removed. Concealed spaces, through which there may be a circulation of air, should be avoided as far as possible, as they act as dust collectors. The amount of dust in a building may be very much reduced by filtering the air before it enters from outside. In a dusty neighborhood some such provision is imperative.

In order to reduce as much as possible the number of resting-places for dirt, it is a common practice in hospital construction to provide for rounded corners at the junction of two wall surfaces, or of wall with floor and ceiling, thus avoiding a right angle. Where this can be done in some stable material, such as plaster, cement, or iron, it is an excellent plan, and makes the labor of cleaning much less. If constructed of wood great care must be taken in the execution, lest cracks and crevices, caused by the shrinking of the material, frustrate the aim of the designer.

In the selection of materials of construction those of a porous, absorbent, or perishable nature should be avoided. Wood, on account of its absorbent properties, and its expansion and contraction under varying hygrometric conditions, should be used as sparingly as possible.

The walls should be designed with a view to their function as a protection against the weather rather than proportioned for strength alone. If of brick or stone the material should be selected for its non-heat-conducting properties chiefly. Both the inside and outside faces of the wall should be rendered as far as possible impervious to moisture.

The body of the wall may well be made of several thicknesses of hollow brick (which is a good non-conductor of heat), and the outside faced with a dense hard brick, of minimum absorptive power. The wall may then be plastered on the inside with a hard, cementitious plaster, smoothly finished, and applied directly to the masonry, without furrings of any kind.

The interior partition walls may be of brick, terra cotta, or metal lathing, plastered on both sides.

Ventilating-ducts and flues, where they are built into the walls, should be constructed of some smooth material, such as fire-clay flue-liners, and the alignment should be as straight as possible. Such flues, as ordinarily constructed in brick walls, with rough interior surfaces, accumulate quantities of dust, which from its inaccessibility is not easily removed.

The framing of floors and roofs may be of rolled iron or steel beams, with fire-clay arches, and the ceilings plastered without furrings.

If the roofs are flat, they must be made of sufficient thickness and of such material as to be a sufficient protection against the heat of summer and the cold of winter. There are many excellent coverings for flat roofs in the market.

For the corridors, toilet-rooms, and offices, the flooring may be of asphalt, marble "terrazzo," or other impervious material. Such a floor, however, would be unsuitable for the rooms occupied by the sick, unless artificially warmed. For these the flooring may be of wood, of the best quality, and laid in the best manner, in default of any better material.

If such permanent fire-resisting forms of construction

are out of the question on account of their greater cost, and it is decided to build of wood, the solid open "mill construction" should be used, as being far superior to the ordinary combustible methods of wood construction. In this case the framework of the building may be of well-seasoned hard pine columns and beams, with outside walls of 3" pine planking, grooved and splined, covered with clapboards, shingles, or Portland cement, and plastered on the inside on metal lathing, which will do away largely with cracking of the plaster. Such a wall is a far better protection against the weather than a thin brick wall constructed in the ordinary cheap manner.

The interior partitions may be, as above, of metal lathing, plastered on both sides, and the floors and roof of 3" planking, with the ceilings plastered on metal lathing. Provision should be made for deadening the floors to the passage of sound. This may be done by inserting several thicknesses of thick sheathing-felt between the planking and the upper flooring.

Such a construction is "slow-burning," there are no concealed spaces, and the defects of wood as a material are minimized.

Especial care must be taken in designing the framing to dispose the material in such a manner as to prevent cracking of the plaster surfaces by unequal shrinking of the wood.

The heating and ventilating systems are so mutually related that they must be considered together. In our northern climate dependence must be placed on some method of artificial ventilation during the greater part of the year. There are also many days, even in summer, when natural ventilation by doors and windows is insufficient. If the ventilation is to approach perfection there must be means of moistening, cooling, and filtering the air. It is also especially important that the temperature of the air supplied to different rooms should be under easy control from the rooms themselves. Furthermore, every portion of the heating and ventilating systems, especially the air-ducts and flues, must be easily accessible for cleaning.

There is a great variety of systems of heating and ventilation. The one which seems to best meet the requirements of a hospital is the so-called "plenum system," in which the movement of the air is effected by a fan or blower driven by mechanical power.

In this system the outside air is taken in at one or more definite points, filtered, cooled, moistened, or heated, according to the requirements of the day, and then forced, through a ramifying system of conduits and flues, to the various points where it is wanted. The air may receive a further addition of heat in its course to the different rooms, varying in each case according to the particular need.

The supply of air, from its entrance to the building to the points of distribution, is under perfect control. By varying the speed of the fan the amount of air supplied may be increased or decreased, and by varying the amount of heating-surface or by the use of mixing-valves the temperature may be controlled without changing the amount of air supplied.

Outlet shafts for the foul air must be built for every room, whatever system of ventilation is employed. But with the power-fan in operation every such shaft will draw well, whereas with other systems they must often be artificially heated to make them work.

Such shafts or conduits should take the shortest and most direct course to the outer air, and not be carried any great distance within the building itself, so that the foul air may be got outside of the building as quickly as possible.

It is a good plan to provide open fireplaces, both for the cheer they give and also as a resource in case of temporary failure of the regular system of heating.

For the plumbing nothing but the very best is suitable for a hospital. The fixtures should be simple and substantial. All plumbing devices of a complicated nature should be viewed with suspicion. Plumbing fixtures in connection with sick-wards should be isolated, so that odors may be cut off.

The above are but a few of the considerations which should govern hospital building. The reader who desires to pursue the subject further may consult the following books:

Notes on Hospitals (Third Edition). FLORENCE NIGHTINGALE. London, 1863.
Hospitals: their History, Organization, Management, and Construction. W. GILL WYLIE, M.D. New York, 1877. (This excellent book is unfortunately out of print.)
Hand-book for Hospitals, No. 32. State Charities Aid Association. New York, 1883.
Hospitals and Asylums of the World. HENRY C. BURDETT. London, 1891.
Healthy Hospitals. Sir DOUGLAS GALTON. London, 1893.
Hospitals, Dispensaries and Nursing. Baltimore, Johns Hopkins Press, 1894.

Description and Plans of a Small Hospital.

The accompanying plans are an attempt to put into a concrete form the "permanent hospital building," the special needs and requirements of which have been enumerated in Chapter VIII. It is assumed that an ideal site has been secured, with ample room for future extension. The plan (see Plate I) shows a lot of about six acres in extent, bounded by a street on one side only. It will be observed that each building is in plan a simple rectangle without wings, L's, or re-entrant angles. The buildings are grouped in alternate succession on opposite sides of a corridor, which is the avenue of communication between them. This arrangement leaves the ends of the buildings free and insures an end-to-end ventilation of the wards. The axis of the corridor lies northwest and southeast. All of the buildings, except the *Administration Building*, are but one story high, with a basement, and all have flat roofs, the under side of which forms the ceiling of the room below. The roofs are rendered non-heat-conducting by a covering of pine planking four inches in thickness.

The *Administration Building*, which occupies the centre of the group, is two stories high. This plan supposes a hospital laundry and a nurses' home in separate buildings outside, and is the ideal arrangement; but if land is too valuable the *Administration Building* may be built three stories high, with a laundry on the top floor (the least objectionable location), and rooms for the nurses on the second floor. By this arrangement the *Nurses' Home* and the *Laundry* build-

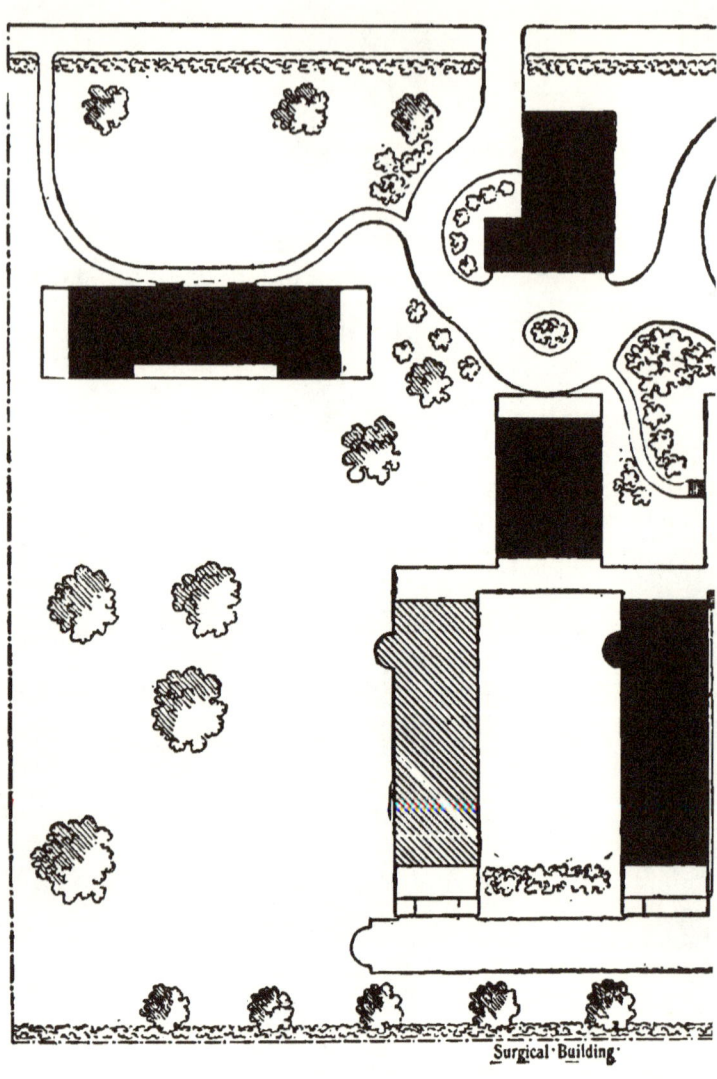

Contagious Ward · Boiler House, Morgue and Horse Sheds · Surgical Building · Ward · Ward

PLATE I.

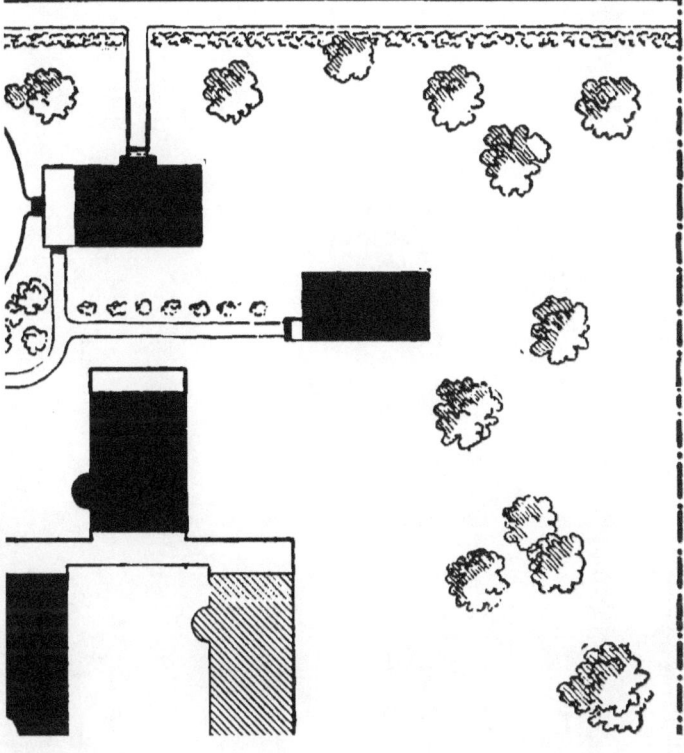

ings could be dispensed with. It is much better, however, to provide for these separately, as shown upon the plan.

The corridor is to be left open in warm weather. In winter it is to be closed in with glass sufficiently to afford protection to the nurses on their way back and forth.

The *Administration Building*, which, from its greater height, casts more shadow than the ward pavilions, is placed so that its shade falls during the greater part of the day clear of the other buildings.

The capacity of the hospital may be increased by continuing the corridor in either direction and adding extra wards. Two such wards are shown in shaded lines upon the plan. (See Plate I.)

The buildings occupied by the sick are furthest removed from the street; and the least agreeable buildings of the group from their associations, the *Contagious Ward* and the *Morgue*, are placed where they are least likely to be seen by the patients. The *Morgue* is furthermore concealed by being combined in a group with the *Boiler-house* and *Horse-sheds*. A separate entrance from the street, with high wall and gate, is provided at this point, hidden from the other buildings, for the entrance of coal-teams and for the hearse.

The horse-sheds are commanded from the windows of the *Administration Building*, so that the doctors may be relieved of all anxiety concerning their horses.

The ward pavilions are composed of two portions, the *Main Ward*, and its service-rooms. The body of the building, containing the *Main Ward* and the *Sun-room*, rises above the rest of the building about four feet. The break thus made in the roof allows of a

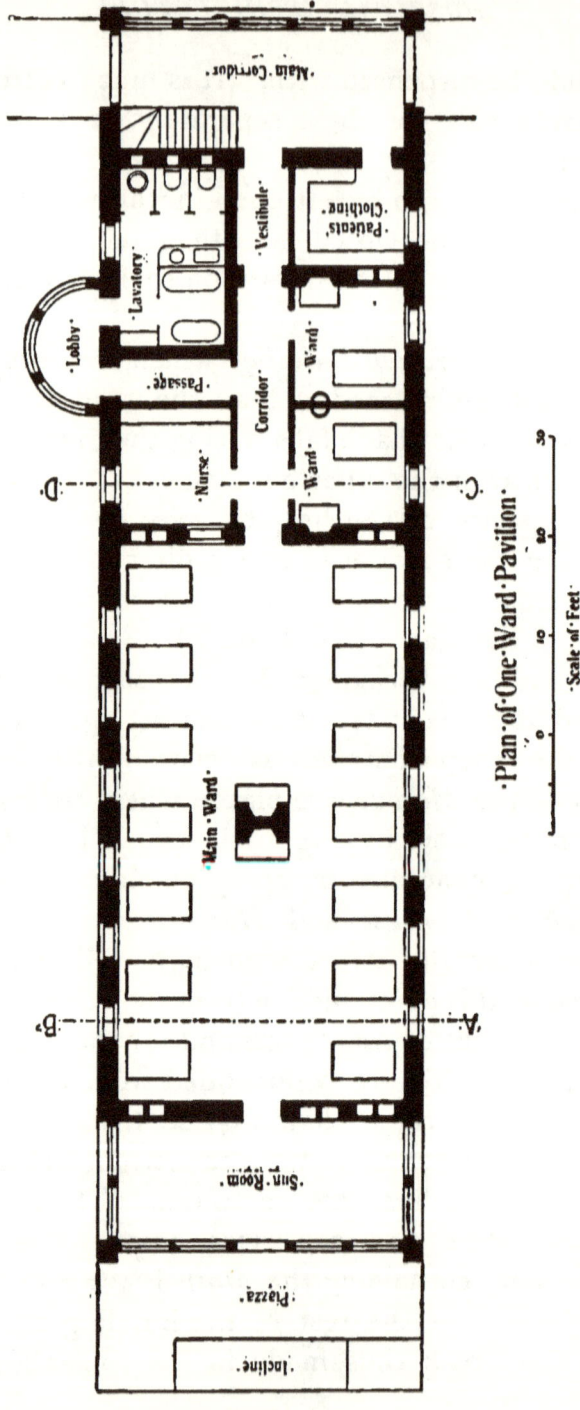

window high up at the inner end of the main ward, thus giving an end-to-end ventilation. (See Plates II and III.)

The *Main Ward* accommodates 14 beds. In the centre is a chimney with two open fireplaces. At the southern end is a *Sun-room* with glazed sides, and beyond this a platform with an *Incline*, so that patients may be wheeled down onto the turf.

The dimensions of the common wards are as follows:

Height of ward............ 14 feet.
Width   "   " .... 30 "
Length "   " .... 56 "
Lineal bed space..........   8 "
Floor space for bed........ 120 sq. feet.

In connection with the main ward are two isolation rooms, 11' 9" × 11' 9", each with an open fireplace. Opposite is a room for the nurse, with a window commanding the ward. The plumbing fixtures consist of a sink, a slop-hopper, a hand-basin, two water-closets, and two bath-tubs, one of which is portable. They are cut off from the rest of the building by solid partition walls which extend down through the basement, and are reached by way of an outside semicircular *Lobby* built out from the north wall of the pavilion. This *Lobby* has three large windows, which are always to be left open a few inches, even in winter, to secure a constant passage of air across. The plumbing fixtures, though under the same roof, are thus as effectually isolated from the ward as if built in a separate tower or annex. The room in which the plumbing is contained is lighted from above by a large skylight through which the sunlight comes. The floor and walls are impervious, so that the whole apartment may be washed down with a hose. There is a large room for the storage of patients' clothes, with a door opening onto the outside corridor. In front of each pavilion the width of the *Main Corridor* is increased to twelve feet. There is a stairway giving access to the subway below. The two ward pavilions are duplicates of each other.

The general floor level of all the buildings is about six feet above grade. This secures the privacy of all the rooms, and gives a light and airy basement.

To the southeast of the *Administration Building* is the *Private Ward*, a pavilion containing five patients' rooms. These are 11' 9" × 13' 9", with an open fireplace in each. Each of these rooms also has the sun. The isolation of the plumbing is effected in the same way as in the common wards above described. (See Plate IV.)

The *Contagious Ward* (see Plate V) stands at some distance from the other buildings. It consists virtually of two separate hospitals under one roof. A solid partition wall divides the building in the middle. The wings containing the patients are one story in height; the central portion of the building, containing the rooms of administration, is two stories in height. The building accommodates eight patients in separate rooms. The plumbing is isolated by an outside platform, and the second floor (see Plate VI) is reached by outside stairways.

On the opposite side of the *Administration Building* from the *Private Ward* is the *Surgical Building* (see Plate VII). This contains the most important room in the hospital, the operating-room. A *Corridor* eight

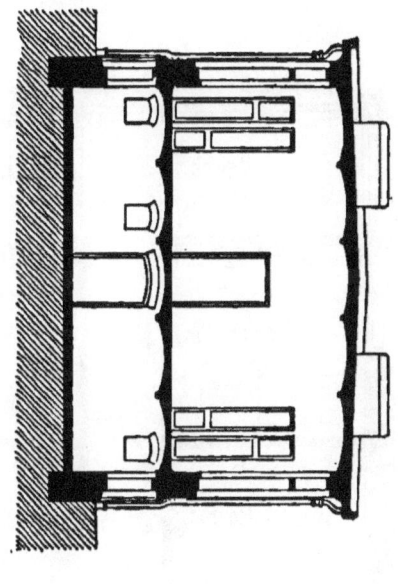
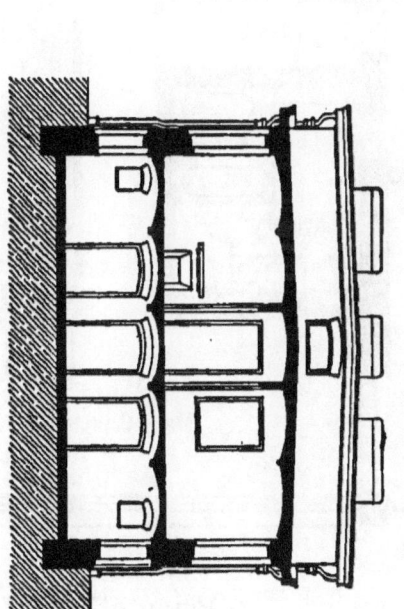

WARD PAVILIONS.

PLATE III.

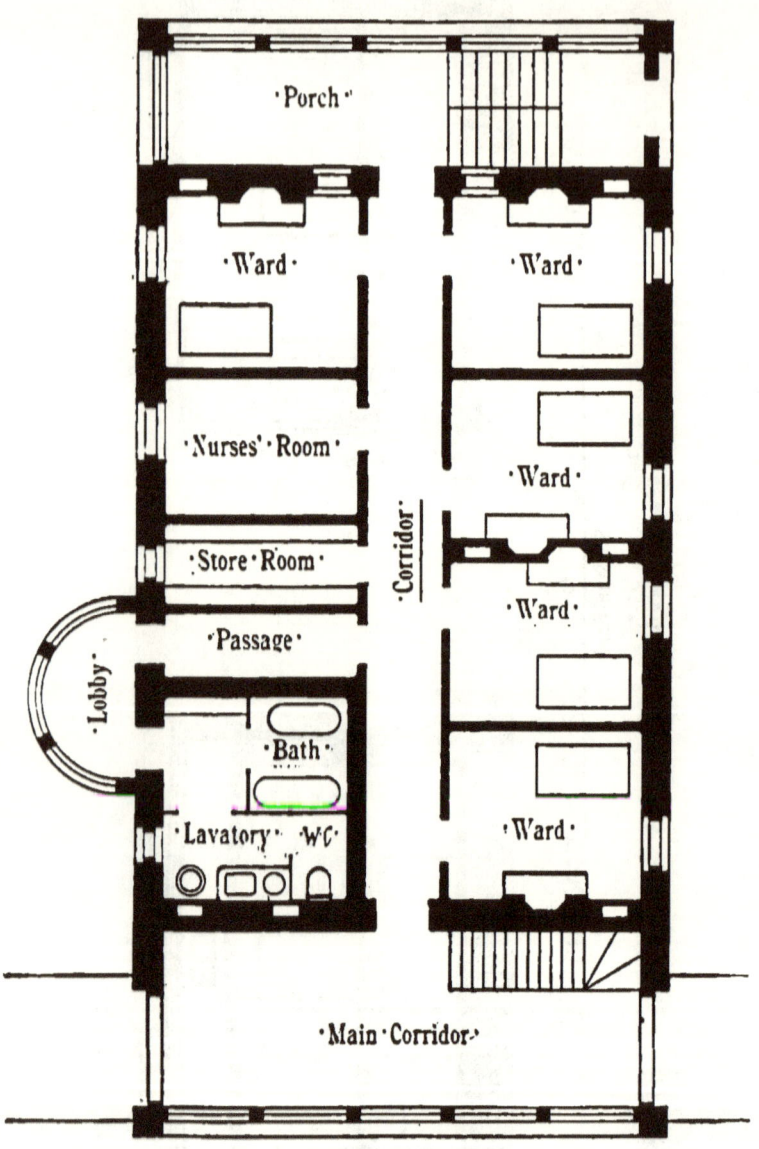

"Private Ward"

feet wide runs through the building from end to end. Patients enter the building from the *Main Corridor* and are taken directly into the *Etherizing-room*. When everything is ready they are taken across the corridor into the *Operating-room*. This room is absolutely bare. Everything necessary for an operation is brought in on glass tables and taken out again as soon as the operation is over. The floor and walls are impervious, and the floor drains to the centre. There is a window on the northwest wall and extending without a break as a skylight half-way back into the ceiling. Just across the *Corridor*, directly opposite, are two rooms, a dressing-room for the surgeons and an instrument-room.

For the reception and treatment of accident cases a separate room is provided, which is a duplicate of the *Operating-room*, but with the addition of sinks, hand-basins, and instrument-cases. There is another etherizing-room opposite. At the other end of the building is the *Sterilizing-room*, also provided with sinks and hand-basins. There are two *Recovery-rooms*, with sunny exposure, for patients after operation. At the north end is a covered *Porch*, for the reception of patients from the ambulance.

The *Administration Building* (see Plate VIII) is two stories high above the basement. Visitors enter a large *Hall*, which also serves as a waiting-room. This hall is entered from a *Vestibule* from which on one side opens the *Office* and on the other side a room for the janitor with circular stair to the basement. Opening off the hall is the doctors' *Library*, and beyond this a room for the head nurse.

The *Dining-room* is of ample size, and has a *China*

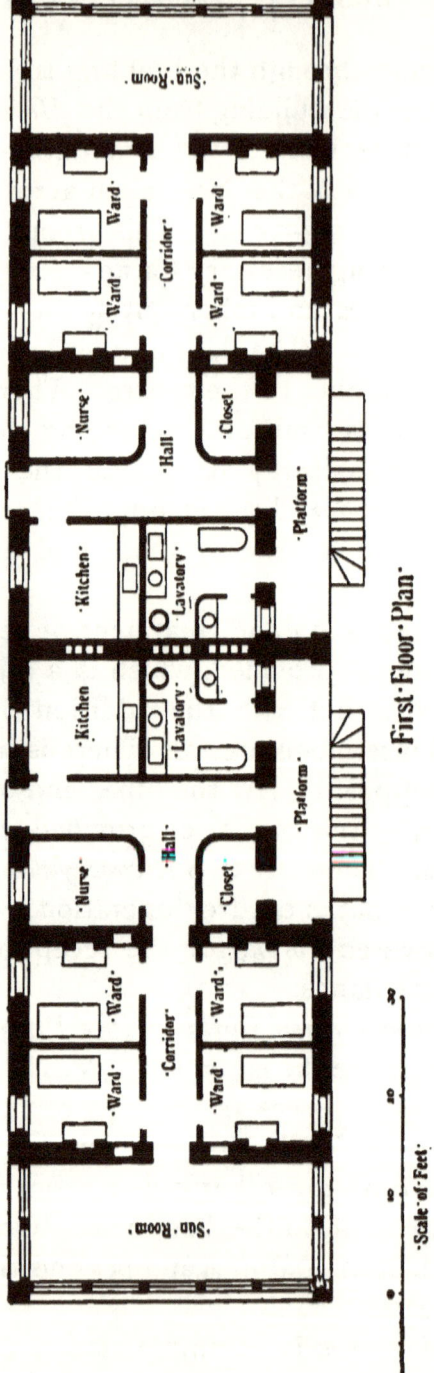

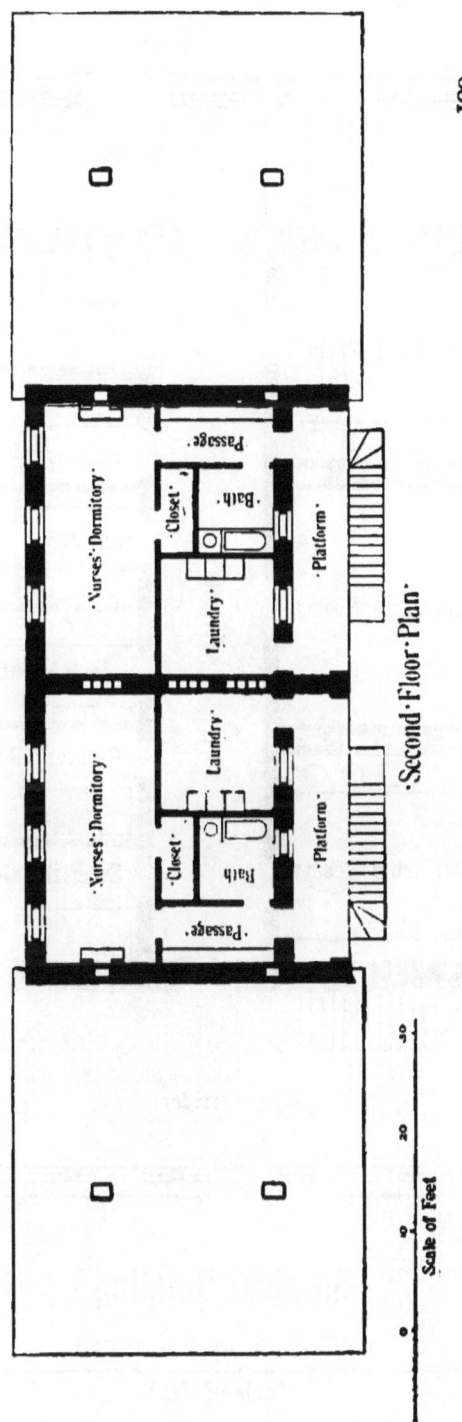

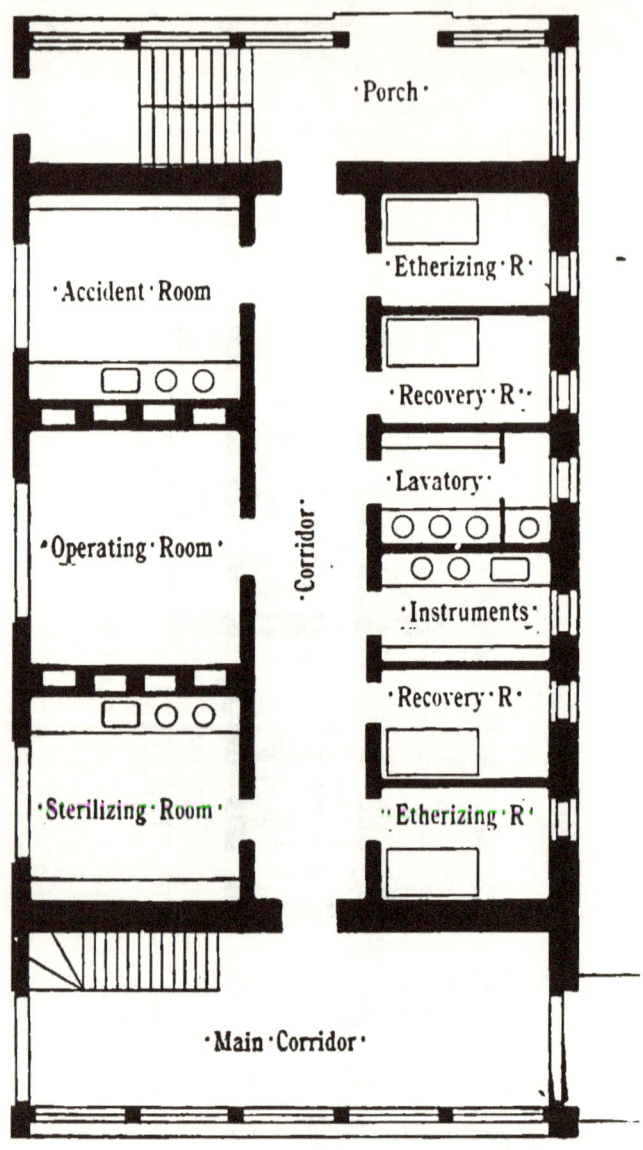

Closet with sink for washing dishes. The *Linen Room* has the sun nearly all day long. Beyond this is the *Nurses' Parlor*. Opposite is the *Tea Kitchen*, which is the depot from which the food is served to the various wards and also to the *Dining-room*. There is a dumb-waiter service to the floor above. From the *Office* there is a private passageway to the *Rear Hall*, giving quick communication to the wards. Off this is a toilet-room for the nurses.

On the second floor is the *Kitchen*. (See Plate IX.) Communication is had with the basement by a large *Lift* on which supplies are brought up. In connection with the *Kitchen* is a *Scullery* communicating with the *Tea Kitchen* below by a dumb-waiter. All the tableware for the sick-wards (excepting the contagious ward) is kept here, and here the patients' meals are prepared and sent down to the tea kitchen to be distributed.

On this floor is the *Matron's Room*, with bath-room adjoining, and a *Spare Bedroom* for visitors. Opposite are two large bedrooms for servants and a separate room for the cook. A large bath-room for their use is provided.

The *Hall* is abundantly lighted from a skylight overhead, and the staircase is continued up to the roof.

The basement of the *Administration Building* contains a cold-storage room for provisions, bins for the kitchen coal and for the wood or coal for the open fires, and a toilet-room for the janitor.

The steam-boilers for the heating apparatus may also be placed in this basement, but it is better, if it can be afforded, to locate them in a separate building outside, as shown on the plan. (See Plate I.)

Under the *Main Corridor* is a subway, about six

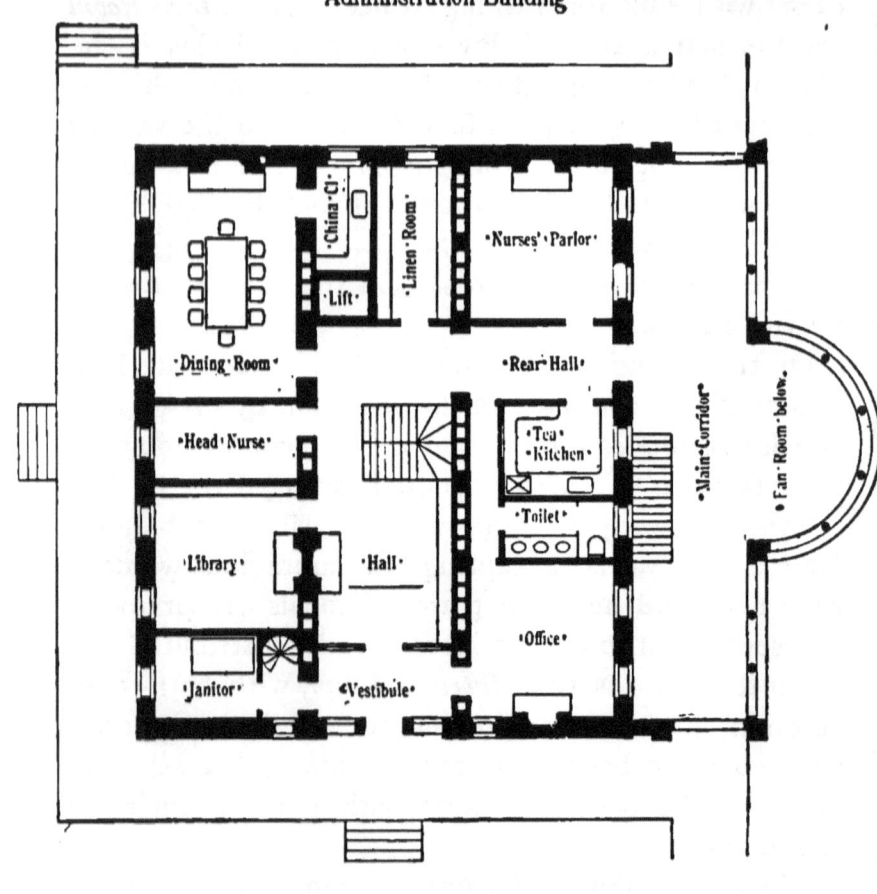

PLATE IX.

Administration Building

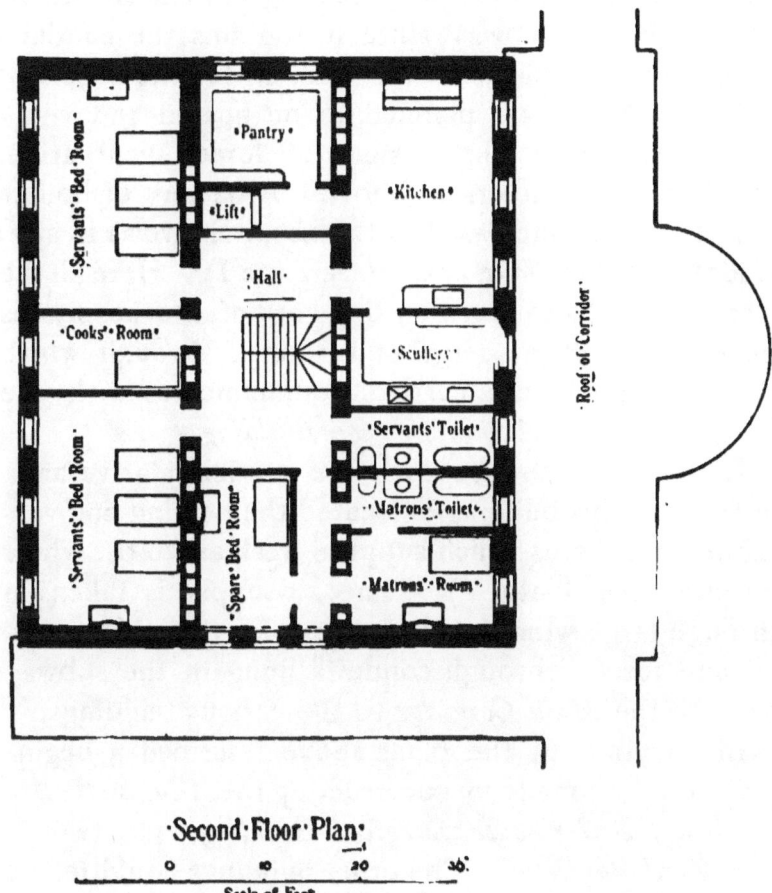

Second Floor Plan
Scale of Feet

feet high, in which are placed the hot-air conduits, hot and cold water pipes, gas-pipes, and electric wires. No portion of the waste-pipe plumbing system should be allowed in this subway, since it contains the conduits through which passes all the fresh air for the hospital.

The buildings are planned to be heated and ventilated by the plenum system of forced ventilation, which has been described above. A battery of boilers (which may be increased as the hospital grows in size) is located in the *Boiler-house* (see Plate I). Here all the steam required to carry on the work of the hospital is generated. An underground tunnel, through which the steam-pipes are carried, communicates with the basement of the *Administration Building*.

In the *Fan-room* beneath the semicircular veranda in front of this building is located the heating and ventilating apparatus which supplies fresh air to the whole hospital (see Plate V). The air-supply is taken in through large windows in the periphery of this veranda and forced through conduits hung in the subway beneath the *Main Corridor* to the various buildings.

In carrying out the plans above described a beginning could be made by constructing the *Administration Building*, *Boiler-house*, *Surgical Building*, and two of the *Ward Pavilions*. The other buildings could follow with the growth of the hospital.

The plan as described provides for 45 beds—two ward pavilions of 16 beds each, a private ward of 5 beds, and a contagious ward of 8 beds; and by adding the two extra pavilions shown in dotted lines the total becomes 77 beds.

www.ingramcontent.com/pod-product-compliance
Lightning Source LLC
Chambersburg PA
CBHW020125170426
43199CB00009B/646